Contents

Acknowledgements

I am indebted to a vast number of people, without whom this book would not have been possible.

First to Laura Dobbs, Mary Springer and all the other lacemakers and teachers from whom I have gained expertise and inspiration. Particular thanks go to Mary for all her patience and encouragement and for convincing me that I could teach. To Chris Buckland of North Dorset Adult Education who gave me my first class. To Alison, my daughter, without whose patience this script would not have been possible. To Pete Beal for taking such good photographs. To Iona Thomas for reading the script. To Gill Forest for information and help with photocopying. To my students in Wiltshire and Dorset for working the prickings, making suggestions and greeting the whole idea with such enthusiasm. Lastly, to my husband Don, a lace widower in the best tradition.

I am also indebted to many companies and organizations which, with one or two exceptions, were amazingly generous with their help. One, in particular, lent me a large parcel of books and paid the postage in both directions.

Information about Linen – Hanna and Co. of Belfast; Barbour Campbell Threads Ltd of Lisburn; Ulster Crafts of Wexford.

Information about Cotton – Madeira Threads (UK) Ltd of Thirsk; Tootal Craft of Manchester; J.P. Coats Ltd of Glasgow; DMC Creative World Ltd of Leicester; Copley Marshall and Co. Ltd of Huddersfield; George Wigley and Sons (Nottingham) Ltd.

Information about Silk – J. & E. Piper of Glemsford, Suffolk; The European Commission for the Promotion of Silk, London.

Information about Pins – Gloucester Museum; Newey Goodman Ltd of Tipton, West Midlands; Whitecroft Lydney Ltd of Lydney, Gloucester.

Information about Downton Lace – Salisbury Museum, Mrs Mary Gibson and Ms Susan Hartley; Wiltshire Records Office; Wiltshire Local Studies Office and Dr John Chandler.

Information about Beads – Linda Mowat of Pitt Rivers Museum in Oxford; Carole Morris of 'Spangles'.

Thanks to Jane O'Dea, Ann Pring and Kathleen Shanks for supplying addresses around the world.

Introduction

Bobbin lacemaking is a wonderfully therapeutic hobby. The concentration required for the work and the delight in the finished piece pushes all other worries and problems into the background. Once one is hooked it is a subject of many facets. Besides all the different styles of lace that it is possible to learn, there is the background of the subject, the equipment which has been used in the past – old bobbins and old pillows, old lace and its identification, the way in which lace was used for costume and how fashion changed. There are museums with collections of lace to be visited. There are also European countries, where lace is made, to be visited. There are fellow addicts to be met in classes, groups and lace days.

I hope this book will be useful on many levels. In the first part of the book I have covered equipment and some background history, followed by a chapter on threads and their construction.

The second part of the book is concerned with Torchon lacemaking. Torchon is an ideal lace for beginners because it is geometric and the pins used in the construction are widely spaced, allowing the lacemaker to locate and rectify mistakes with ease. It is also a stepping-stone to making other types of lace. There are twelve patterns which introduce most of the motifs from which Torchon is designed, in a variety of combinations.

At first, emphasis is placed on written instructions but, with growing confidence, the lacemaker should gradually be able to read details from the photograph of the lace for a particular pattern and follow a numbered diagram. There is advice on mounting lace in a variety of ways. This is followed by information about changing the scale of the lace by using different grids and a variety of threads. Nearly all the lace has been worked with white thread so that it will reproduce clearly in the black and white photographs. I have nothing against coloured lace and have made suggestions about using colour in the text. There are some prickings which lacemakers can in part design themselves, and advice on drafting patterns which may appeal and for which no pricking exists or for which no corner exists.

There are suggestions about how pieces of lace may be used and advice on recording and storing lace. There is some advice on finding a teacher and lists of useful addresses for lace suppliers and museums which have lace collections. Chapter 13 gives a variety of grids and graph papers, which could be used for designing Torchon lace.

1 Lacemaking Equipment

Lacemaking can be a hobby to suit all pockets. The main essentials are a pillow which holds pins firmly, some covers, bobbins to hold the thread, card for the patterns (called prickings in lacemaking), pins in vast numbers and thread. To this can be added a list of useful items which are in no way essential. I would advise spending the minimum until you are sure that bobbin lacemaking is for you.

PILLOWS

For a beginner I would recommend a mushroom-shaped pillow of polystyrene. These pillows are available relatively cheaply, not at amounts to make you feel out of pocket if you do not take to lacemaking. If you have a choice, opt for one which is fairly flat on top. Depending on progress and the type of lace in which you become interested you can then move on to any of a variety of shapes of pillow or even commission one yourself for a particular project. Inevitably, if you get hooked you will want a second or even a third pillow.

Eventually the polystyrene will become soft and no longer hold pins firmly. It can be given a new lease of life by purchasing a set of blocks intended as replacements for a block pillow. The blocks can be placed on top of the pillow and their outline marked with a felt pen. This outline can be excavated with a craft knife (best done out of doors to avoid poly-

styrene chips around the house) until the blocks fit neatly into the space and are approximately flush with each other and the outline of the pillow. I placed my blocks in an L-shape because I was afraid that a channel across the pillow would split its base. The blocks could have been hidden under the pillow cover. However, I pressed the cover into the excavated hole, put the blocks above it and had a block pillow at comparatively small expense. Although the blocks cannot be shunted about, the whole pillow and individual blocks can be turned as necessary.

Although a mushroom pillow is very suitable for beginners' work and small pieces of lace, it is not the most convenient shape for doing lengths of lace because the lace will need to be moved up the pillow, a somewhat nerve-racking experience. This problem can be avoided with a different though more expensive type of pillow.

French Pillow

This type of pillow has a roller around which the pricking is pinned and the lacemaker works round and round until the required length is achieved. The roller fits into a shaped base on which the bobbins are spread. This type of pillow is not suitable for working edgings with corners.

Block Pillow

This type of pillow is suitable for con-

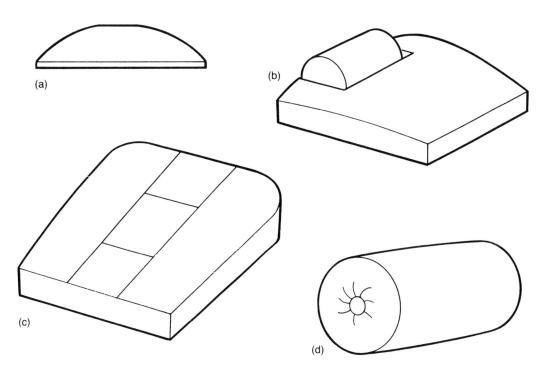

A variety of pillows. (a) mushroom pillow; (b) French pillow; (c) block pillow; (d) bolster pillow.

tinuous lace and for pieces with corners. It is also suitable for curved pieces and collars. These pillows come in a wide variety of sizes and designs but consist of a base holding a series of blocks. The blocks can be shunted up the pillow as work progresses and the top block removed and placed at the bottom. The blocks can also be turned for working corners. With forethought they are also suitable for collars. It is always wise to go through the movements of the blocks for a particular pricking to see that the work can be carried out. In some pillows it is possible to work across the blocks and their base. In other pillows the blocks sit in a trench with wooden sides which will not take pins. When the blocks wear and become soft, they can be turned over and lace can be worked on the reverse side. When the second side is too soft a new set of blocks can be purchased.

Bolster Pillow

This type of pillow is a cylinder shape and should be at least 11in (28cm) in diameter. The greater the diameter the larger the flattish area will be at the top of the pillow. The lace is worked around the pillow and this style of pillow is more suited to the short Bucks bobbins. Some lacemakers do not feel comfortable working on this type of pillow but they were used in vast numbers in the past.

Modern pillows are made either in the traditional way with chopped straw, or with polystyrene or allied products;

sometimes a combination of the two is used. The straw-filled pillows need chopped straw which has to be packed and battered and malleted and packed again until it is rock hard. In use it will probably soften and need repacking. As a result of all this labour, straw pillows are more expensive to buy than polystyrene ones but last longer.

Both types can be made at home. Scrap polystyrene can be obtained from shops selling refrigerators and other large electrical goods or scavenged from the dustbins of such shops. It can be cut quite easily into blocks which can be covered with calico or some other suitable fabric. For a straw-filled pillow a calico or hessian case is needed and in the case of a mushroom or French pillow a plywood or hardboard base. The straw is packed in to capacity and the space in the case is sewn up. Lacemakers become very ingenious if their pockets are not deep.

The traditional pillows of the East Midlands, historically one of the chief lacemaking regions, were the round or bolster pillow and the so-called 'square' pillow which had its corners rounded off. Both types, packed with straw, were heavy and cumbersome and required the 'horse' for support. Old photographs of lacemakers show these types of pillows very clearly.

In Downton the bolster pillow was used. In Devon a smaller round pillow was used because Honiton lace requires frequent changes of direction in the working of the lace. In Spain and Malta a pillow

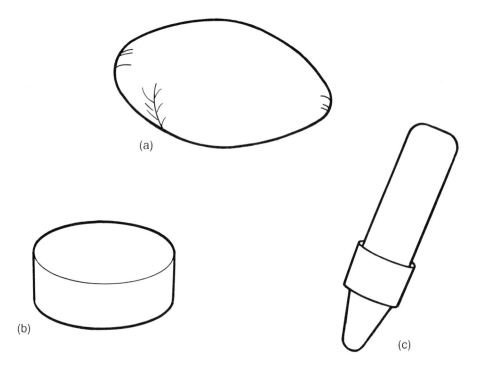

More pillows. (a) square pillow with rounded corners; (b) Honiton pillow; (c) pillow from Malta and Gozo.

rather like a chunky French loaf was used. One end, which was tapered off, fitted between the lacemaker's knees. The other end rested on the back of a chair or door frame. The lace was worked in narrow strips down the length of the pillow which rested at quite a sharp angle. These strips were later joined together to make larger items like shawls and collars. This type of pillow can still be seen in use in Gozo. The French pillow was rarely seen in this country and even scorned as a 'drawing-room pillow'. Some were sold as 'Torchon pillows'.

COVER CLOTHS

Some mushroom pillows are supplied ready covered. If this is not the case you will need a round piece of fabric about 25in (64cm) in diameter. This must be hemmed and elastic or a draw tape threaded through the hem. The fabric must be drawn up and neatly tied on the flat underside of the mushroom. Wear and tear on the pillow can be cut a little by putting a piece of felt or padding on the curved surface of the mushroom before placing the cover. You will also need one or two hemmed rectangles of fabric with which to cover your working surface.

The fabric for all these covers should be of darkish blue or green, which are the most restful colours to the eyes. These are also the traditional colours. The fabric should be lint-free so that loose fibres do not get worked into the lace. If you are on a shoestring budget it is sometimes possible to get suitable off-cuts of sheeting from market stalls.

Traditionally three cloths were used, one under the pricking, one at the top of the pillow over the finished lace and one at the bottom of the pillow over the pricking and under the bobbins. The purpose of this one was to stop the threads catching on the pricking. When work was not in progress this cloth could be folded back over the work to keep it free of dust. These covers have such regional names as 'drawter' and 'heller'. It is important to keep lace clean and it must be remembered that an uncovered pillow will gather as much dust as the mantelpiece. All these covers can be washed between projects.

Bruges flower lace involves working in many different directions with many pins pressed into the pillow. The lacemakers use a cloth which covers the pillow and has a round, faced (as in dressmaking) hole in the middle. The bobbins are spread on the cloth but the pricking and pushed-in pins are all covered except in the working area. This saves threads from being caught on pins. A cloth of this type is useful for small mats and motifs.

On the Continent some areas use cover cloths of soft leather lined with fabric. In some countries brightly coloured and patterned fabrics are used.

LACE BOBBINS

Bobbins are pieces of equipment on which the lace thread can be wound and held under tension while the lace is worked. As these pieces are needed in vast numbers for even narrow pieces of lace it seems logical that a thin stick shape should have developed. The shapes of these 'sticks' do vary considerably according to the country in which the lace is made and the type of thread used for that lace.

In England, Honiton, Downton and

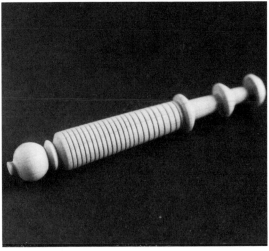

'England's oldest bobbin?'

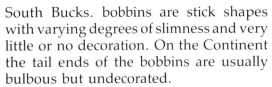

Bobbins. Left to right: Continental; Bucks Thumper; Downton; Honiton; plastic East Midlands.

South Bucks. bobbins are stick shapes with varying degrees of slimness and very little or no decoration. On the Continent the tail ends of the bobbins are usually bulbous but undecorated.

It is the shape and decoration of East Midlands bobbins which are of greatest interest and delight, not only to lacemakers but also to collectors who see them as an investment. They are an example of everyday objects of 150 years ago becoming collectable and worth money. The East Midlands bobbins are of two types, those which are classed as antique dating from the nineteenth century, and modern copies.

The earliest known bobbins, however, date back to the end of the seventeenth century. Bobbins were made of bone or hardwood. Fruit woods were popular. The wood had to be close grained to turn well. Sometimes they were whittled and

given as love tokens in the manner of Welsh love spoons. One such bobbin, dated 1693, is in Salisbury Museum. It has a painted decoration and is chunkier than their earliest Downton bobbin which is dated 1789. Gloucester Museum has a bone bobbin found in a rubbish pit which was part of an archaeological dig in Eastgate Street in 1974. The pit is thought to have been in use between 1680 and 1750. It is unlikely that it was new when it was thrown in the pit so it is possible that it is England's oldest bobbin and owes its survival to its bone origin. A wooden bobbin would have rotted in the intervening years.

While considering the inclusion of a line-drawing of the bobbin, I discovered that Carole Morris of Spangles supplied a replica in hornbeam called 'England's Oldest Bobbin?' The photograph is included with her permission. She has written a short article about the bobbin which was published in 1988 in *Lace* Issue 49. (*Lace* is the newsletter of The Lace Guild. Addres-

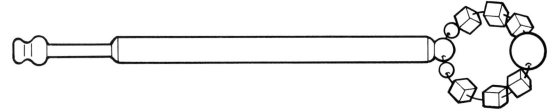

The basic East Midlands bobbin.

ses for The Lace Guild and Spangles are included at the back of this book.)

The trade of bobbin maker existed in its own right at least as far back as the beginning of the eighteenth century. Richard Kent, 'bobbin maker' was buried at Olney in 1728.

This is the first paragraph of an article 'A Note of Lace Bobbins' by Mrs Head in *The Connoisseur*, a magazine for collectors dated November 1904:

'Collecting lace bobbins is a hobby which has, at any rate, the merit of being a tolerably unhackneyed one. Possibly to the uninitiated this may seem its soul claim to interest, but a glance at the array of examples shown here – and they form but a very small part of the collection from whence they are taken – will surely dispel this idea and prove the bobbin's title to rank as an 'object' to be sought after for its own sake.'

Antique bobbins, because they are collectable can be very expensive, especially if they are interesting in some special way. They may look dull and dusty but if actually used for lacemaking they soon develop the lovely sheen of well-cared-for old wood.

The alternative to the antique bobbin is the modern reproduction. With the upsurge of interest in lacemaking as a hobby have come the modern bobbin makers who copy and adapt the old designs. Ten years ago many of these bobbins were badly finished with rough patches on which the thread would snag. However, lacemakers are discerning people and examine design and finish before buying. The result is that standards have risen considerably.

The diagram above shows the basic outline of an East Midlands bobbin. In antique bobbins the shape of the head and tail end are often the 'signature' of a bobbin maker, who may not even be known by name. Only one bobbin maker actually put his name on some of his bobbins. I have two identical bobbins and one is named at the tail end of the shank. It is possible that he marked just one of a set of bobbins. Archibald Abbott lived from 1815–1885 and the name is indented into the wood in the same way that my grandfather, a joiner, had his tools marked with his name. Whether the bobbins were made of wood or bone, similar variations of design were used. Bone bobbins are rarer than wood because they were, and still are, more expensive.

Most of my antique bobbins were given to me by Mrs Colquhoun who used to live in Amesbury and who is now living near Banbury. At the age of 90 she decided she would learn to make lace and that is how I met her. On my first visit she said, 'I've got some bobbins', and opened a drawer to show a lacemaker's dream.

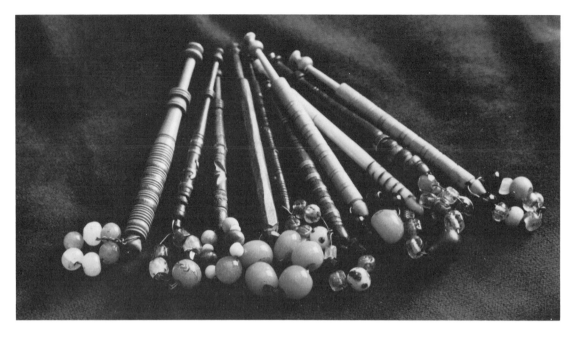

A selection of antique East Midlands bobbins, including a Bedford fly and a jingle. First and fourth from right are Archibald Abbott tigers.

Decorated Bobbins

Turned bobbins Simple or elaborate turning, either straight round the shank or spiral. Bone bobbins were sometimes dyed.

Bitted bobbins Usually dark wood bobbins inlaid with small pieces of light wood although occasionally light can be found inlaid with dark. The inlay was held with glue and sometimes came unstuck.

Tigers Decorated with bands of colour or inlaid with bands of pewter.

Leopards Decorated with spots of colour or inlaid with spots of pewter. These bobbins are rough to touch and are said to help arthritis.

Jingles Loose rings of wood or pewter on the bobbin shank.

Fairings These were sold at fairs. A fine spiral was cut into the bobbin. This was filled with a strip of tinsel held in place with brass wire.

Wire-wound bobbins Fine brass wire wound round the shank in a variety of ways, both straight and spiral, to make a pattern. Sometimes seed beads are threaded on the wire.

Bedford fly Arrow-shaped pieces of pewter inlaid into the shank.

Mother and babe A small bobbin running loose inside the pierced shank of the bobbin.

Lantern Small beads enclosed in the pierced shank.

Church window An empty pierced shank.

Cow and calf or jack in the box The hollowed shank pulls apart to reveal a small bobbin similar to that in a mother and babe.

Inscribed Bobbins

The inscriptions were made as a series of dots, either straight or as a spiral, which had to be turned anti-clockwise to be read. Bobbins inscribed with Christian names were most popular. Many were biblical names, some of which seem old-fashioned today. Sometimes the names were misspelt. Sometimes the names were prefixed by Dear or Sweet. Sometimes there was a surname and less often, a date. Some commemorated births or deaths or, in the case of a young person, both.

I have already mentioned whittled bobbins as love tokens. Another group of love tokens would have been ordered with suitable inscription from the bobbin maker. Such inscriptions as 'Forget me not', 'I love you my dear that is true' and 'Nothing but death shall part us too' were common. Spelling was not always perfect.

Commemorative Bobbins

Bobbins sometimes celebrated an event of national or local significance like a hanging or an election. Election bobbins were distributed by the candidates to gain support. Hangings were public and hanging bobbins were distributed to commemorate the event. Today these are much sought-after and valuable. As a result there has been talk of forgeries. Recently a collection of bobbins was presented for auction at Christie's in London. They had very lengthy inscriptions which led to questions of authenticity – which in turn led to their withdrawal from the sale.

Modern Bobbins

The modern bobbin makers use all the aforementioned designs. Modern inscriptions may be more relevant: 'I'll clean the house tomorrow'. Local events like Lace

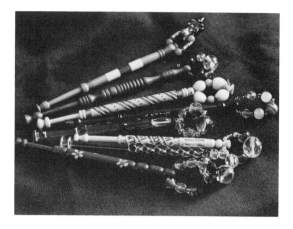

A selection of modern reproduction bobbins including a lantern and a mother and babe.

Days or fund raisings are celebrated. Museums with lace collections often sell inscribed bobbins.

National events like Royal weddings and births, elections, the Falklands War and the raising of the *Mary Rose* have all been celebrated on bobbins.

After the big hurricane of October 1987, bobbins were made from the wood of uprooted trees and sold in aid of tree-planting charities. One maker added a red and green glass apple tree as a spangle on each of his charity bobbins. As I write, the anniversaries of the Second World War are being commemorated – Dunkirk, The Battle of Britain and so on.

Bobbins can be commissioned, so some lacemakers have their own family history in their bobbin collection. They can also be commissioned for presentation to others.

Beginners at lacemaking can start with plastic bobbins, the cheapest type available, and gradually build up a collection of antique and modern bobbins according to their taste and pocket. The purists frown on plastic but if any material serves the purpose of holding the thread without snagging I see no harm. A smooth plastic bobbin is far better than a rough wooden one.

Making your own bobbins

If time and patience permit, bobbins can be made from dowelling.

Materials

Dowelling — ¼in (6mm) diameter or a length that feels comfortable
Small saw
Sharp knife
Very fine sandpaper and flour paper
Fine drill bit

1. Cut lengths of dowelling.
2. Using a manufactured bobbin as a guide, mark the position of the area to be cut away. Place the knife on the dowelling and roll it across the working surface, applying firm pressure.
3. Whittle out the wood which is not required, making sure you do not cut too deeply. (Best done out of doors!)
4. Use the sandpaper and flour paper to smooth the surface and to round off the top and the bottom of the bobbin. Make sure there is no roughness to catch the thread.
5. Use a fine bit to make a hole for the spangle.
6. Rub with a dab of wax polish.

Refinements

1. Dye the wood with potassium permanganate solution.
2. Varnish with coloured varnish. (Wood dye alone is no good as the colour will transfer to the thread.)
3. Decorate with a poker-work tool.

4. Decorate with a soldering iron which has a fine tip.
5. Whittle a more elaborate pattern.

Many modern bobbin makers started with dowelling for a wife, moved to friends and acquaintances, bought a lathe and started a small business. Besides the nationally known names there are many bobbin makers known only in their own locality and these are all worth investigation. Craft galleries are often worth a visit.

SPANGLES

East Midlands bobbins are a delight not only for the great variety of shape and decoration of the shanks but also for the spangle of beads or souvenirs with which their tail ends are decorated. No other area or country has decorated bobbins in this way.

'Spangle' is a term used to describe the item or items on the tail end of a bobbin. Most often this is a ring of beads but these come in such variety that no two bobbins are ever identical. The earliest spangle dates from the beginning of the nineteenth century.

The reason for the development of the spangle is not known though it has been suggested that when machine-spun cotton was introduced the bobbins had a greater tendency to roll than with the less highly twisted hand-spun thread. Spangles do stop the bobbins rolling on the pillow. The thread may also have needed extra tension which the weight of the spangle would have provided.

Continental bobbins have bulbous ends which give weight. Honiton is worked with fine thread which does not need great tension and the techniques are such that spangled ends would be very inconvenient to the working of the lace. Downton lace is worked in a Continental manner with fine threads and South Bucks. bobbins, although not bulbous, are quite chunky in design.

There were four ways in which the spangle was attached to the bobbin.

Staple This was probably the oldest method of spangling. A pin minus its head was bent round and both ends hammered into the tail of the bobbin and the spangle hung on this staple. The head of the pin was often hammered into the head of the bobbin. As the pins were made of brass they must have looked even more attractive when new and shiny.

Hinged This was the rarest method because it was the most difficult and so reserved for special bone bobbins when the spangle was an integral part of the design. A wedge was cut in the tail of the bobbin, a pivot pin fitted across and the spangle suspended from the pivot.

Drilled A hole was drilled in the tail of the bobbin. The lacemaker could thread beads on a wire, pass one end of the wire through the hole and twist it with the other end to form a ring. The wire could

then be trimmed and the ends pushed between two beads so that they did not catch in the lace. Brass or copper wire was used. For best effect the hole had to be drilled at a right angle to any inscription so that when the spangle was in place, the design showed to best advantage.

Shackle This method made use of a drilled hole. A pin or piece of wire was passed through the hole and twisted to form a loop. The spangle was assembled and strung on this loop.

Spangles were usually made of beads, and nine seems to have been the most usual number though this could vary. More than twenty have been recorded but today the most usual number seems to be seven.

The nine consisted of one large 'bottom bead' or 'centre bead', three square-cut beads on each side of it and a small round bead on each side of the bobbin tail, sometimes called the closing bead. To this ring could be added souvenirs or sentimental bits and pieces. Sometimes the spangle was made entirely of objects other than beads.

Birdcage spangles were also made. These consisted of a large bead surrounded by bands of small beads in the

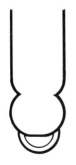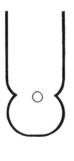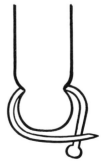

Ways of attaching spangles.

Modern birdcage spangles.

manner of a bird cage. The wire on which the small beads were threaded tended to corrode and so few examples have survived.

Bead Manufacture

The earliest known glass beads date back to 1500 BC and were found in Egypt. This is hardly surprising since glass is made by using great heat to fuse a silica with an alkali. Sand is a silica found in large quantities in Egypt. Other possible silicas are sandstone, quartz and flint. The alkali elements could be soda or potash and were obtained by burning vegetable material. Soda could be made from glasswort and seaweed, and potash from bracken and ferns.

The components of the glass depended on the area of manufacture and the resulting glass had different characteristics. That from soda made a glass which was easy to manipulate and which when molten could be pulled out to a silk-fine

filament and cut with scissors. This type is traditional in the Mediterranean. Glass made from potash which was more suitable for cutting and engraving was traditional in northern Europe and led to cut-glass industries in various parts of the UK.

Although the Egyptians had perfected many bead-making techniques and had spread their knowledge so that beads had become a high art form by Roman times, the art disappeared in the Dark Ages. Eventually it was reintroduced to Venice from the Near East to be a well-established and highly organized industry from the thirteenth century. In 1292 the industry was moved to the island of Murano, three miles from Venice, because of the fear of fire in such a highly populated area. It has been there ever since.

A visitor to Venice in 1730 stated that several streets were inhabited entirely by people making and stringing beads which 'The women of the lower class wear about their necks and arms as ornament'. The work was specialized and the makers were named according to the type of beads they made, thus *Margaritai* made small beads, *Perlai* made larger hollow beads and *Paternostreri* made rosary beads. At first, glass-making was a rather hit-and-miss process with success by luck and experience. As knowledge of chemistry grew, a more reliable product could be made.

Colouring beads was a skilled job. To a certain extent they depended on impurities in the original ingredients. These colours could be altered by the addition of further ingredients and controlled heat. Cobalt was used from earliest times to produce various shades of blue, probably because lapis lazuli was highly prized.

Copper produced turquoise, green or red glass according to the furnace and both turquoise and cornelian (a reddish colour) were prized. Tin oxide produced opaque white glass and could make other colours opaque.

Once the glass was made, beads could be manufactured in a variety of ways. The molten glass could be wound on to a wire to the correct size and, while still molten, shaped with various tools or decorated with the addition of thin filaments or spots of different colours. These beads with added glass could be heated to fuse the colours 'in relief' or 'marvered' (rolled on a marble or iron surface) to give a smooth symmetrical shape. Many beads had a combed thread decoration. The threads of contrast glass were wound round the bead and then dragged across the surface with a sharp object in the manner of feather icing.

'Mille fiori' beads were decorated with chips of glass of many colours in the manner which was later associated with paper weights. 'Eye' beads date from 1000 BC and were originally bluish-black with white or yellow spots embedded in them. Much later we had the 'Kitty Fisher's eye'. The bead was grey with red and blue spots on white in the rough arrangement of a face. Kitty Fisher was a famous actress of the mid-eighteenth century, mistress of Sir Joshua Reynolds and subject of many portraits by him and others. She and Lucy Locket were said to be 'ladies of easy virtue'. Glass surfaces were sometimes painted, enamelled or gilded. All the beads discussed so far are of the type used as the bottom bead of a spangle.

The type of bead which occurs most often on old bobbins is the square cut. The molten glass has been pressed into a cube shape with a file and has a characteristic dimpled surface. They are usually transparent pink or clear, though blue, green and yellow square cuts have been known.

The other main method of production was the pulled bead. Air was blown into the molten glass which was then pulled out to form a tube of the required diameter. This tube could be cut into beads the required length. Alternatively the cut pieces could be placed in an iron container with sand and charcoal and rotated in a furnace. This method was used to produce round beads.

Beads were easily transportable, and for centuries were used for trade and barter with the tribes of Africa, the American Indians and the inhabitants of the East Indies. The Pitt Rivers Museum in Oxford has a collection of trading bead samples. These suggest that different shapes and colours appealed to different cultures. Very tiny beads were popular with North American Indians who wove them into braids which decorated their clothes and tools. Any exhibition of North American Indian artifacts includes bead braids of traditional patterns although they were also influenced by European styles. I recently saw some beadwork which reflected the Victorian taste in flower decoration.

Many designs were tied up with superstition which supposedly gave them magical power. Blue was thought lucky and animal harnesses were often decked with blue beads to make them sure-footed. 'Eye' beads were to ward off the evil eye.

As Britain was a great trading nation it seems likely that she imported beads from Europe to re-export them from the great trading ports of Bristol and Liverpool. It seems that some of these beads stayed here and found their way into lacemakers' bobbins. However, lacemaking in this country was a cottage industry, carried out by people who probably could not read or write, so its history has been oral rather than written. Oral history, written down comparatively recently, tells us that beads were made by blacksmiths who had the furnaces and could use scrap glass. Some were said to be made by bobbin makers and there is evidence in trade directories that this is true. On the other hand, Linda Mowat of the Pitt Rivers Museum tells me that many of the beads in their bobbin collection were made in Venice, Bohemia and Moravia. She recommends L.S. Dubin's *The History of Beads*, which I have been unable to track down. For those interested in more information, The Bead Society of Great Britain the appropriate organization (*see* Useful Addresses, page 169).

Rosary beads and beads of other materials are sometimes found in spangles. Wooden beads were sometimes plain and smooth, sometimes carved, and sometimes of yew, which was supposed to give protection from accidents. A wide variety of other objects were used with or instead of beads on spangles. Buttons seem to

have played an important part in the superstitions of lacemaking. A group of buttons could serve the same purpose as the evil eye beads and ward off mistakes. Whereas we regard unpicking our mistakes as part of the process of learning, to a lacemaker it was money lost for time wasted in unpicking and reworking and the possibility of dirty work and rejection by the laceman who did not have to buy the work.

Modern Ways of Attaching Spangles

It is a good idea to collect beads. Look for items at jumble sales. Ask friends for broken necklaces. Swap with other lacemakers to get a wide variety. Buy beads which you find attractive at lace days or from bead specialists. Consider the colour and decoration of the bobbin to be spangled. Select a bottom bead and three pairs of beads of graduated size in a suitable colour and arrange them in order. Choose brass or copper wire which is flexible but not too fine, or the spangle will squash out of shape.

A variety of antique spangles.

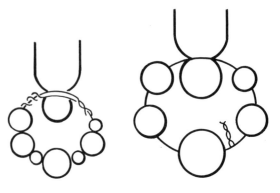

Modern ways of spangling.

PINS

In lacemaking, pins are needed in very large numbers because they are used to hold the thread in place on the pricking as the work progresses. A beginner could use any dressmaking pins which happen to be at home.

The big danger for lacemakers is rusting of the pins. Any corrosion on the surface of the pin, which may not even be obvious, will be deposited on the threads as the lace is worked. Rust marks are difficult to remove. The second danger with corrosion is from pins in a pillow which is damp or sits in a damp atmosphere. As the pins corrode the thread can become embedded in the corrosion and break when the pin is removed.

When an investment in new pins is necessary the lacemaker can feel overwhelmed with the vast choice in a good haberdashers or lace suppliers. Newey and Scovill are the names most often associated with pin supplies. Neweys are most often on display in haberdashery departments and Scovills appear in suppliers' lists.

Basically the choices are over the metal and size. Brass is the traditional metal for lacemaking pins because it does not rust, although it can become tarnished. Brass can be identified by its gold colour but some brass pins are nickel plated giving them a silver colour. The disadvantage of brass is that it bends very easily. This is particularly the case with the finest pins. Pins of equal fineness are available in stainless steel. These do not bend as easily as brass and are highly resistant to corrosion. Neweys sell these pins as 'Wedding Dress and Lace Pins'. Dressmaking pins are made of nickel-plated steel and are more prone to corrosion.

There are two sizes which usually appear on packs of pins, the first is the length of the pin and the second is the thickness of the pin. The sizes are imperial or metric or both. The length of pins varies from 1in (26mm) to 1⁵⁄₁₆in (34mm). The thickness of pins varies from the finest 0.021in (0.53mm) through 0.024in (0.60mm) to 0.026in (0.67mm). . Brass 'Wedding Dress and Lace Pins' at 0.021in (0.53mm) thick are suitable for fine work. Dressing pins at 0.024in (0.60mm) thick are probably more suitable for coarse work but be aware of corrosion.

Besides the conventional style of pins with a small head, there are also available ranges of pins with coloured plastic or glass heads. A few of these are useful for marking the stage you have reached in your work or for holding groups of bobbins away from the current area of work. Hat-pins can be used for the same purpose. Fancy hat-pins are highly collectable and expensive but are often found among the belongings of elderly ladies. Most of my collection came from my grandmother.

Investigation into the historical aspects of pins gives opposing views. A variety of lacemaking and sewing equipment books state that until the seventeenth century pins had to be imported from France and were very expensive. As a result thorns and, in coastal areas, fine fish bones were used. By contrast in a leaflet entitled *The History and Origins of Pin Manufacture* by Newey Goodman Ltd, it states that in 1400 the Duchess of Orleans purchased from John Breconnier '500 de la façon d'Angleterre' indicating that pins were exported to France at an earlier date. There was a Guild of Pinners in London in 1356, and in 1543 Henry VIII set standards for the quality of pin production.

During the first quarter of the seventeenth century, pin manufacture became well established in the Bristol and later in the Gloucester area, as employment for workhouse paupers. Between 1608–1626, 1,500 people were employed in Bristol alone and a Protection Act forbidding 'the import of pins except by the pinners themselves' was passed.

The site of Gloucester Folk Museum in Westgate Street was once a pin-making factory. During archaeological excavations in Gloucester from 1974–81 several hundred pins dating from the mid-seventeenth century to the early eighteenth century were found. Of these, sixty-eight were complete and suitable for examination, and it was found, by plotting graphs of length against diameter, that there was only crude control of pin length, though shorter pins were manufactured from narrower gauge wire than longer pins. It also appeared that the Standard Wire Gauge introduced officially at the end of the nineteenth century to standardize pin diameter was already in use. The pins found ranged from ¾in (19mm) to 1in (25mm) in length and from 0.5mm to 1mm in diameter, the shorter pins being at the finer end of the range. Among the other artifacts found at the excavation was the lace bobbin already mentioned on page 10.

In 1663 the Ryland family started a small pin-making business in Birmingham. With the arrival of the Industrial Revolution in the eighteenth century, Birmingham developed as an important centre of engineering. The stage was now set for the development of pin-making in Gloucester and Birmingham, a situation still existing today with Whitecroft Lydney Ltd of Lydney, Gloucester, selling under the name Scovill, and Newey Goodman Ltd of Tipton, West Midlands, selling as Newey.

In 1765 Adam Smith, in his book *The Wealth of Nations*, identified eighteen distinct operations for the production of a pin. By using eighteen men, one to work each stage instead of one skilled man to work all of them, he was able to increase pin production from 20 pins per day per man to 4,800 pins per day per man. The pin industry is an example of a milestone in industrial development.

The earliest pins were made with a separate head which was not very securely fixed. Solid-headed pins were first sold in London in 1833. The detachable head made it possible for lacemakers to decorate their pins in various ways. They used small beads, sealing wax, or burrs. The burrs could be soaked in milk or vinegar depending on the desired colour. They would swell, making it possible to remove their skins and the burrs could be slid on to the pins. As they dried they tightened on the pins making a secure head. As with other equipment there were local names for these decorated pins. They were 'bugles' in south Buckinghamshire, 'limmicks' in north Buckinghamshire and 'king pins' in Bedfordshire. They were also called 'strivers' because they were put in the lace as a gauge of the speed of the worker. Speed of work was important. Children in lace schools were expected to put up ten pins per minute, 600 pins per hour if they were to escape the teacher's cane.

Lace 'tells', which were really working chants, were sung to move the work along. Many are similar to the traditional nursery rhymes we learn as children. 'One, two buckle my shoe', was probably one such rhyme. 'Five, six pick up sticks' could refer to bobbins.

Today Newey Goodman Ltd can list fifteen types of pins for different purposes using a variety of metals of different gauges. The industry produced about nine billion pins in 1982, 65 per cent of which were exported. It is an industry keen to make use of and serve technical development. New alloys which are more resistant to corrosion could be useful to the clothing and dressmaking trade. 'Ball point' pins have already been designed for jersey-type fabrics. Although lacemakers use comparatively few pins from this industry we can always select what may be to our advantage in any new development. I have been told that in France some lacemakers use entomological pins in their work.

PINCUSHIONS

When making lace it is more convenient to have your pins in a pincushion on the pillow than in a box which could be knocked over. The pincushion should

A pincushion holding hat-pins, brass pins, berry pins and strivers. (Strivers kindly given to me by Jane O'Dea.)

not occupy too much space and can be held in place by a hat-pin or pinned by a loop of ribbon.

Heart shapes are quite traditional. To-day we often decorate these with a narrow edging of lace. A stuffing of emery powder will keep the pins smooth and sharp. The greasiness of a bran filling will keep them smooth. Honiton pin cushions are traditionally stuffed with unscoured sheeps' wool so that the lanolin will keep the pins smooth.

PIN LIFTER

This is a small implement which serves two purposes. There is usually a small indentation in the end of a handle which can be used to push pins into the pillow. On the other end will be a two-pronged metal implement which will fit around a pin and lift it from the pillow. This is not an essential piece of equipment but saves wear and tear on finger tips and finger nails. Something can usually be improvised. In America they sell a dimpled metal ring, like an open-ended thimble, for pushing pins into the pillow.

SMALL SCISSORS

Scissors to cut lace threads must be very sharp to give a clean unfrayed cut. Do not allow them to be used for anything else.

LIFTING PAD

A lifting pad is a device to help move the lace on the pillow, if the whole pricking is too big to be worked in one go. I usually use strips of felt to form a graduated stack.

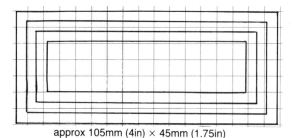

approx 105mm (4in) × 45mm (1.75in)

Lifting pad.

PRICKINGS

Lace patterns are called prickings. In the past they were called parchments. I have read that parchments were made of pricked vellum. Parchment is the inner part of sheepskin prepared for writing and painting, while vellum is the inner part of calfskin also prepared for writing and painting. These materials were gradually replaced by a very tough glazed card.

Today the ways in which prickings can be made give rise to controversy. Whatever the pros and cons, good lace cannot be made with a poor, inaccurate pricking.

PRICKER

This is a tool with which to make prickings. It is a needle held in some form of handle. The thickness of the needle should bear some relation to the thickness of the pins to be used. Too thin a needle will give the lacemaker sore fingers. Too thick a needle will allow the pins to wobble and distort the lace. A 'pin vice' makes a good handle. There are also a wide variety of holders of different designs available from bobbin makers and specialist suppliers. The simplest device is made by cutting the pointed end from a needle

and sticking the cut end into a piece of dowelling. About ¼in (5mm) of the point should protrude from the wood. Making a pricking can be time consuming so it is important that the pricker feels comfortable when gripped between the fingers.

BEESWAX

Stabbing the needle end of the pricker into beeswax periodically helps it slide more easily into the pricking card. The beeswax can be bought in blocks or in small, turned wooden pots.

IMPLEMENTS FOR MAKING SEWINGS

When joining lace it is necessary to pull a thread from a bobbin through a loop in the lace. This can be done in several ways.

A latchet hook is a first choice for many people. Latchet hooks for dealing with snagged threads on clothing are available from haberdashery departments. These are suitable for coarser types of lace. A much finer latchet hook is available from

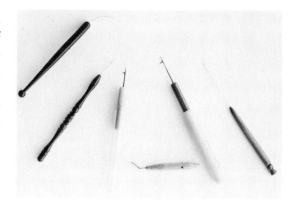

A variety of tools for making sewings.

A reproduction bobbin winder, kindly lent by Iona Thomas, and a modern nylon bobbin winder. The bobbins are in position for winding.

specialist suppliers. Some people manage very well with a fine crochet hook.

For Honiton lace the traditional implement is a needle pin. This is a needle in a wooden handle with the point of the needle facing outwards. A modern variation of this has the eye of the needle outwards and the needle bent at an angle. This is called a bent needle pin. A more flexible beading needle is sometimes used and sold as a 'Lazy Susan'. The best method for each lacemaker can be found by trial and error. They all take a little practice.

BOBBIN WINDER

Bobbin winders are something of a luxury, although they do save time in winding bobbins for a large project. They are of two types. Reproductions of old designs made of wood and beautifully finished to make attractive house ornaments, and the nylon or steel variety which clamp to a table. The reproductions work on a wooden wheel and elastic band principle and the actual designs are as varied as those of the past. The clamp types work in much the same way as a hand drill from which they are adapted. The bobbin fits where the drill bit would be and as it turns the thread is wound on to the bobbin.

Antique winders had an extra part which we do not need today. The thread was sold in skeins. The skein was stretched around four pegs fitted into two crossed blades of wood. These crossed blades turned on a spindle as the thread was wound. These winders were called 'turns', a very appropriate name for their purpose.

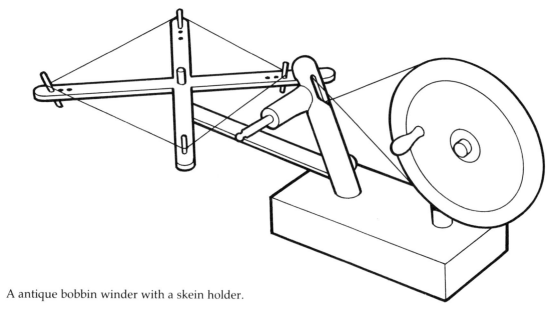

A antique bobbin winder with a skein holder.

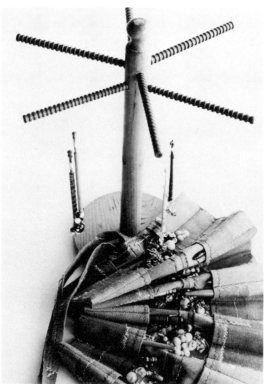

A bobbin bag and bobbin tree. (The tree was kindly given to me by Barbara Price and made by her son.)

BOBBIN BAG

To avoid the inevitable knotted thread, pairs of wound bobbins need to be stored separately from one another. An oblong piece of fabric can be folded and stitched with a series of narrow pockets into which pairs of bobbins will slide. When not in use it can be rolled up and tied with tape. Bags of various designs can be bought from specialist suppliers or designed and stitched by lacemakers to their own specifications.

BOBBIN TREE

This is a device rather like a mug tree but with longer, straighter arms which have grooves cut in them. Wound pairs of bobbins for immediate use can be hung on the tree until they are taken into the work. When not in use the bobbin tree should be covered to keep it free from dust.

TRANSPORTING A LACE PILLOW

When lace is not being made the pillow should be kept covered and in a place where it will be safe and secure. A pillow tipped over and tangled is a heartbreaking occasion.

Many lacemakers attend classes or groups and this involves carrying the pillow. The bobbins should first of all be pinned down under a strip of ribbon, tape or elastic, making sure that pins are not stuck into the pricking. A cover cloth should be folded over the pillow covering the pins in the pricking. The body part of a pair of tights can be slid over the bobbins as an extra precaution. The pillow can now be placed on a square cloth and opposite corners knotted over the pillow. Alternatively it can be slid into a purpose-made bag with the bobbins hanging vertically downwards. Again bags of various designs and levels of sophistication, with the addition of pockets for other equipment, can be bought or made. Pillow bags and bobbin bags can be bought or made to match.

2 Threads

Traditionally, lace was made of threads produced from natural fibres of animal or vegetable origin.

The main animal fibres were wool, from various animals, and silk. The vegetable fibres were linen and cotton, though fibres were and still are produced from other plants and were as varied as pina cloth from the pineapple plant and pine wool made from the leaves, bark and cones of the Scots pine. A recent fashion article in a glossy magazine had photographs of two very expensive embroidered shirts, one of pineapple fibre and one of banana fibre. These threads, each with their own individual properties, were used to make lace of traditional style and colour. A name like Chantilly will conjure up a picture of black lace even to someone who is not a lacemaker.

Much lace was white, but the Victorians wore large quantities of black lace because Queen Victoria was in mourning for such a long period. By contrast the Edwardians had a great fondness for ecru-coloured lace, a colour which they often obtained by dipping the lace in tea or coffee. Bright colours were used to some extent on the Continent, notably in Russian lace.

The folklore on lace threads is that only natural threads bed down well and hold their shape in the lace after the pins are removed. Man-made threads such as nylon are constructed in a way which discourages them from forming a shape unless that shape is set in with heat, as in pleated skirts and trouser creases.

However, man-made threads are still being developed and their characteristics improved, and at the same time there is a trend towards being more creative in lace-making.

This creativity has been going on for several years and with the development of the new City and Guilds lacemaking qualification in Britain, with its emphasis on original design, it is likely to go even further. Though there is nothing wrong with working the old traditional patterns many lacemakers have the urge to develop new ideas and now they are able to do so with official approval. It is acceptable to experiment with any fibre and any colour or combination of colours and the results are often a delight to behold.

WOOL

Wool is the coat or fleece of the sheep, of which there are many breeds. At the appropriate time of the year, this fleece is removed by a process called shearing. The resulting bale of wool is graded so that the best use can be made of it.

Wool grows in much the same way as hair and is the waterproof coat of the animal which is very greasy. It is also dirty and filled with foreign substances like twigs and burrs. The first process in production is scouring. This removes the grease and much of the dirt. The grease, or lanolin, is collected as a valuable by-product. The wool is then dried and

A sheep.

crushed so that solid impurities are reduced to a powder which will drop out.

The wool is now ready for carding. This process combs the fibres of wool so that they all fall in the same direction, and sorts short fibres from long ones. The short fibres are then spun or twisted into wool yarn. The long fibres are spun into worsted which is a much finer, smooth-surfaced yarn.

Fine wool has been used for many years to make knitted lace like Shetland shawls and other garments. It is also widely used for crochet. If a pricking of appropriate size is designed, Torchon lace techniques can be used to make garments such as scarves and shawls. The shawls are usually made of strips of lace which can be joined together to form the required shape. Man-made yarns which have the appearance of wool can also be used with great success.

History and Identification

Yak was a type of Torchon lace which was made in the past. It was introduced in 1870 and used to trim garments for chil-

dren. The white form had a dull appearance but coloured forms were shiny. Very little survives because wool is prone to attack by moths. Wool is also more difficult to work than linen and cotton. Some woollen lace was produced in Le Puy.

SILK

The origins of silk are to be found in the Far East and date back 4,000 years. The Chinese Empress, Hsi Ling, is said to have discovered that the cocoons on her mulberry trees were made of a fine fibre which could be unwound and woven into a cloth.

The secrets of silk production – or sericulture – were closely guarded for many years, but with the development of the Silk Road from China to the Mediterranean, over 5,000 miles of very rough country, silk was brought to the West and regarded by the merchants who carried it as a commodity as valuable as gold and precious stones.

The Emperor Justinian is credited with introducing smuggled silkworm eggs into Italy in the sixth century, so breaking the Chinese monopoly. Silk production con-

A silk moth.

tinued and is still regarded as a luxury. The word 'silk' evokes richness. It is listed in household accounts and wardrobe bills of the great houses along with the items of lace. These documents, together with contemporary portraits, give us a good idea of their style and colour. A list compiled in 1600 gives detail of items of 'Silke' in the wardrobe of Elizabeth I.

This luxury fibre is produced by the silkworm, which is more accurately the caterpillar stage of the moth *Bombyx mori*. The moth lays eggs which pass through the usual lifecycle of caterpillar, chrysalis, adult moth. The caterpillar feeds on mulberry leaves for three or four weeks, growing very rapidly and shedding its skin three or four times. Eight thousand silkworms will consume 350lb (113kg) of mulberry leaves during this stage of their lifecycle and produce enough silk for ten blouses.

For commercial purposes the worms are reared in trays, so these leaves have to be picked and chopped. This is a very labour-intensive process requiring vast numbers of mulberry trees which need to be pruned and sprayed and kept in good condition. When it has reached the appropriate size the silkworm begins to construct a cocoon by extruding threads from two glands in its head in a figure of eight movement. The threads, fibroin, are coated with a gum, sericin, which bind the whole together to form the cocoon which, when complete, is peanut shaped and just over an inch (about 3cm) long.

If nature took its course the caterpillar would change to a moth within the cocoon and when fully formed, break out, mate and start the cycle again. However, this would break the silk filament and make it impossible to unwind. In order to produce silk the chrysalis must be killed

in a process called stifling, usually using hot air or steam. The complete cocoons are then ready to have the silk unreeled. The cocoons are placed in hot water to soften the sericin, and brushed to find the two threads which have formed each cocoon. These ends are joined with threads from four or five more cocoons to form a complete silk thread with the sericin binding all the filaments together. The thread can be reeled into hanks as a continuous filament, each cocoon being over ¾ mile (1,000m) long.

The filament which is produced by the caterpillar has a triangular shape which acts like a prism, reflecting light and giving the skeined silk its beautiful cream-coloured appearance. The skeined silk is then exported or goes through one of many processes to produce a wide variety of silk fabrics.

The silk used in this country comes mainly from China, Brazil and Japan. It will go to a silk throwing mill, where several reeled threads are put together or twisted in various ways to produce a thread suitable for the weavers. This process is called throwing. There are two throwing mills in Suffolk and one in Leek, Staffordshire. These mills produce yarn mainly for weaving but the mill at Glemsford, Suffolk can produce silk which is suitable for lacemaking and embroidery.

Most silk fabrics are woven from this continuous filament yarn. However, because silk is a precious commodity nothing is wasted. Bits of waste pieces of cocoon which accumulate during continuous filament production are collected, softened, combed out and twisted to form spun silk, which has a smooth texture, and noil silk, which is knobbly and often has lumps in it.

Silk is produced on a small scale in the

UK at the Lullingstone Silk Farm, which is now incorporated with the Worldwide Butterflies at Compton House near Sherborne in Dorset. This English silk has been used for two coronations and various royal weddings. The visitor can see the silk worms at various stages of development and watch the cocoons bob in hot water as the filaments of silk are skeined off into hanks of gleaming pale golden yarn. A video film then shows how this silk is processed to make the silk fabric.

History and Identification

Blonde, Chantilly and Maltese lace are the main types of lace made from silk.

Blonde lace was made from natural silk. It first appeared about 1750 to answer fashion's need for a light, pretty type of lace. The design was of flowers and leaves with a heavy gimp outline on a lightweight ground. It was made in many places from Spain, through France to the East Midlands. This type of lace was later made with black and white silk giving rise to black blonde and white blonde lace.

Maltese lace was a nineteenth-century lace made with a fairly thick thread of natural silk. This meant that it was quicker to make than many other types of lace. The design usually included a Maltese cross and numerous tallies (leaf shapes). It was sometimes made of black silk and both types were popular for shawls, collars and cuffs.

Bedfordshire Maltese lace copied and adapted designs from Maltese lace, and black silk was used for some of these designs.

Chantilly lace was usually black and dates from the mid-eighteenth century. At first it was made with linen but later a dull black silk called grenadine was used. Most designs were floral and the gimp was of thick untwisted silk. Chantilly was widely copied when machines were invented. With the machine variety the gimps could not be worked in the normal manner and this can be an aid to identification. Sometimes the gimps were sewn in by hand which meant they were not held in position by twists in the work. Sometimes they were laid in parallel by machine. There are two cut ends at the beginning and end of each motif.

Silk net was first made successfully when Heathcoat patented his bobbin net machine in 1808. This net could be used alone or embroidered in a variety of ways.

LINEN

Linen is one of the earliest fabrics known to man and its history goes back 10,000 years. It was used by the pharaohs in Egypt, regarded as a status symbol in the Middle Ages and is still seen as a luxury.

It is produced from the flax plant, *Linum usitatissimum*. Flax is a German word, while the Latin name for the flax family is Linaceae. These two terms can cause confusion. In the industry the term flax is usually applied to the plant and its fibres while linen is used to refer to the product made from the flax fibre. Flax is the only natural plant fibre native to western Europe. It is an annual crop which requires good soil and long hours of daylight in warm damp conditions. The growing season, which lasts no longer than 100 days, produces closely grown straight stems about 1m high, which as they mature produce blue flowers and turn rich straw-brown. At the appropriate time the flax is harvested by pulling the

A flax plant.

either in its country of origin or in the country to which it is exported.

Spinning This is undertaken by forty companies in Europe, of which eight are in Northern Ireland and two in Scotland. These companies turn the flax fibres into linen yarn. There are two processes of spinning which can be employed. The dry process, which will produce a coarse yarn and the wet process, which involves soaking the flax fibres in warm water to soften the natural gums, which will produce a fine, regular yarn.

Manufacture of the final product The yarn is spun differently for each different end use, be it weaving, sewing thread, string and twine, webbing or knitting.

Ireland has always been famous for its linen. The industry had its origins in the sixteenth century when Huguenots fleeing from religious persecution brought their skills as weavers to Ireland. Louis Crommelin, an Amsterdam banker and member of a famous Picardy linen trade family was invited to Ireland by William of Orange in 1698 and is regarded as the father of the Irish linen industry.

At this stage it was a cottage industry, very hard work and labour intensive. Scutching and hackling were done by hand until the mid-eighteenth century when small water-mills were built to do the work. From that date the industry gradually became more mechanized and changed from a cottage industry to a factory industry.

John Barbour went to Ireland from Scotland in 1784 and started a thread-making business. Barbour Campbell are still producing threads which are used by lacemakers today, along with those of Bocken from Sweden and Bouc from Belgium.

whole plant to give maximum length of fibre. If seeds are required for next year's crop or to produce linseed oil, a longer growing period is required. The plants are spread on the field or bundled and stooked so that they dry. 'Rippling' is the term given to the recovery of the seeds.

Next, follow five stages in the production of linen.

Retting This is a process of decomposition. The flax plants are placed in tanks of warm water for about five days or laid in the fields for 3–6 weeks to be dew retted. Bacteria break down the gums which hold the fibre to the straw.

Scutching The flax is crushed and beaten to separate the fibres from the woody part of the plant.

Hackling The flax is combed to separate the short fibres from the long ones. The short fibres will be used for tow and to make coarse fabrics. The longer fibres will be used for sheeting and fine fabrics. Nothing is wasted.

These three processes take place in the area where the flax has been grown. The resulting fibre is now ready for spinning,

History and Identification

Lace dates back to the sixteenth century. Until about 1750, when blonde silk lace appeared, all lace was made from linen. The gossamer-fine thread with a count of 1,200 (*see* page 35) was not made after 1800, so very fine lace must predate this time. It was not until 1833 that it was possible to make a cotton thread strong enough for hand lacemaking so cotton lace must date from after this time.

Laces of the sixteenth, seventeenth and eighteenth centuries are of two types. Firstly, needle laces made with a needle and thread using a buttonhole stitch, and secondly bobbin laces made by weaving threads which are wound on to bobbins. Each of these types can again be subdivided by centuries and the areas of Europe in which they were made. Each area developed its own characteristic style of design. Lace identification is a complex subject and can only be learned by looking at lace and pictures of lace and learning from the experience.

The needle laces of these centuries include Reticella and Punto in Aria, English Hollie Point, a number of Venetian Point laces including Gros Point, French Alençon and Argentan, Flemish Point de Gaz and many others.

The bobbin laces, some of which used the gossamer-fine thread, include Binche, Valenciennes and Mechlin.

Needle Laces

Reticella This was a geometric cutwork lace made by buttonhole stitching on a piece of linen and cutting away parts of the fabric to give an open design.

Punto in Aria Translated, this means 'stitches in the air'. It was the next stage in the development of needle lace and was made without a fabric ground. The stitches were made literally 'in the air'.

Hollie Point This was the only English needle lace. It was made with rows and rows of tightly packed stitches with occasional spaces. The design appeared as a series of pinhole-sized dots. Hollie Point was made in narrow strips and used mainly in baby clothes.

Venetian Point These laces had varying degrees of heaviness and padding, Gros Point being the most heavy and almost seeming to imitate the popular wood carving of the time. These laces had no ground (net backing).

Alençon This lace was very light and delicate compared with the Venetian lace and had a light twisted net ground of a round appearance.

Argentan This was another more delicate lace distinguished by its hexagonal buttonholed net ground.

Point de Gaz This was one of the most delicate and expensive laces. Characteristically it had roses with tiers of petals which stood away from the work to give a three-dimensional effect.

Bobbin Laces

Binche This lace was gossamer fine with a haphazard design of holes and straight edges.

Valenciennes This lace developed from Binche but had a much more definite design of flowers and curving shapes. The lace was very delicate and designs were outlined with a series of holes. The edges of the lace were gently curving and there was no cordonnet.

Mechlin This lace had designs similar to Valenciennes but outlined with a thick thread called a cordonnet or gimp.

31

COTTON

Cotton, like silk, was known in the East but only with the development of trade was it introduced into Europe. It was grown and used in India at least 3,000 years ago and gradually spread through the ancient world of the Far and Near East. News of it probably reached Britain in the mid-fourteenth century. Like linen it is most often grown as an annual plant of the family Gossypium but requires the sub-tropical conditions available between latitudes 40°N and 30°S, namely the southern states of North America, Egypt, India, China and parts of South America. It requires moisture and sun during the growing period and the right conditions must prevail at the right time for each stage of its development.

Cotton plants grow from 1ft 6in–4ft 6in (0.46–1.37m) high and produce about twenty beautiful flowers coloured according to the variety of plant. The petals drop in three days, leaving green seed pods. These seed pods or bolls grow and develop over the next two months. They reach the size of an egg, turn brown, harden and split open to reveal a tangled mass of cotton fibres attached to seeds. These fibres are 1–2in (2.5–5cm) long. Harvesting, which may be by hand or machine, must be done at exactly the right time to give the best quality fibre.

In some parts of the world cotton is a perennial plant and trees can reach 15–20ft (5–6m) high. After harvesting the cotton bolls are placed in large machines called gins which separate the fibres from the seeds, stems and leaves. The fibres are also separated, short from long. The resulting cotton is packed into bales and exported to the cotton-spinning and weaving regions of the world.

A cotton boll.

In England the cotton industry developed in Lancashire. This came about for a variety of reasons. The damp climate gave the humidity necessary in cotton manufacture. There was plenty of soft water for bleaching and dyeing and to provide power. There was coal which, together with water, could provide steam power. There were convenient ports for importing raw cotton and exporting finished goods.

The manufacture of cotton involves the breaking open of the imported bales of cotton and the shaking out of the cotton fibres which have been compacted in the bales. The cotton must be carded and gradually drawn out into a long sliver or 'roving' ready to be spun. The cotton is spun and the thread constructed according to its ultimate purpose.

When cotton was first manufactured it had rather a fuzzy, fluffy appearance in use. This led to the development of two different processes to make a smoother thread. Gassed cotton was passed through a coal gas flame to make it less fluffy. This process was patented by

Samuel Hall in 1817. Mercerized cotton was treated with caustic soda which makes the fibres swell and gives the thread a smoother appearance with a slight sheen. This process was developed by John Mercer in 1844.

Cotton, like linen, is used in a wide variety of situations from the fine to the very coarse, from sewing threads to fan belts, from typewriter ribbons to dish-cloths.

History and Identification

It was not possible to spin cotton fine enough for lacemaking until after 1830. Cotton was also rather fuzzy until the gassed or mercerized products were available. Cotton was much cheaper than linen but the lace was of poorer quality. All areas began to use cotton. In this country both Bucks Point and Honiton were made of cotton.

This was the time of the Industrial Revolution and lacemakers were competing with machine-made lace. Heathcoat started making net in 1808, first with silk and later with cotton. This cotton net was gradually taken up by people wishing to make a lace by hand but more quickly than by the traditional bobbin or needle method.

Honiton motifs were appliquéd to machine net.

Bobbin laces were made with a narrow edge of ground, identical in size to machine net, and the two could be joined invisibly.

Tambour lace used a tambour hook to work patterns on net with a chain stitch. Coggershall lace was of this type.

Needlerun lace used a needle and thread to run patterns over and under the meshes of the net. Limerick lace was of

this type and there were said to be more than forty different fillings which could be used with motifs outlined with a running stitch. Tambour lace was also made in Limerick.

Carrickmacross lace used net with a muslin applique. The two fabrics were tacked together and a thick cordonnet thread was couched round the design outline through the net and muslin. The surplus muslin was cut away leaving the design motif applied to the net ground. Needlerun fillings were often added to the design. Net on net lace used a similar design to that for Carrickmacross.

Chemical lace was a machine-made lace. Cotton was used to embroider a pattern on silk. When the embroidery was completed the silk backing was dissolved away with chemicals. Machines were also widely used to copy handmade lace. Valenciennes in particular was very widely copied. Eventually it was possible to copy everything and nearly all these laces were made with cotton. Linen was never used for machine lace.

WHICH THREAD?

You should choose the best available thread for a particular project. All thread should be from the same batch, because the colour may vary.

The choice of thread must be related to the size of the grid on which the pricking is drafted and to the ultimate use of the lace. If a thread is too fine for the pricking, it will not hold its shape well. If a thread is too thick, patches of whole stitch will become wrinkled because there is insufficient space for the threads to lie side by side, and thus good tension will be impossible.

Most patterns state the thread which the designer used. This does not mean you cannot use something similar. Experimenting will increase your experience. As you build a collection of threads it is a good idea to stick samples on a piece of black paper in order of thickness. This means that any new thread you acquire can be graded. Bookmarks and small motifs are good for experimenting with new threads. Make notes so that you can use them for future reference. If beginning a large project, work a sample to see if the chosen thread is suitable.

Cotton

This is the best thread for beginners. A smooth finish and even thickness make it pull into shape well and produce lace with a good tension. It is available in a wide range of sizes but will probably shrink when washed.

Linen

Linen is very strong and durable and will be the best thread for heirlooms like tablecloths. It is not available in a fine count because it would be too expensive to produce. Until recently it was only available as white, half-bleached and ecru. Now some manufacturers are producing coloured thread. It does not shrink as much as cotton. Its disadvantage is that it is not a smooth thread, having slubs and thin patches which will break if you are too heavy handed. Twists in the pattern are sometimes difficult to pull up to give a good tension.

Silk

This is extremely smooth thread which pulls up well to give good tension. The threads will slide about in the work so the right thickness for a given pattern is important if a good finish is to be achieved. Too little thread in a patch of whole stitch will give a poor result.

Smooth hands are important when working with silk as the thread will catch on any roughness and spoil its texture. Natural silk has a beautiful colour.

Wool

Individual yarns need to be used experimentally before starting a project. I have found that some yarns will shrink up considerably when the pins are removed, resulting in a much reduced piece of lace.

THREAD CONSTRUCTION

Threads are manufactured by pulling out the fibres to be used to an even thickness and twisting them. These threads are called singles and have little strength. Two singles can be spun together to form a 'two cord' thread, three singles will form a 'three cord' thread, four singles a 'four cord' thread and six singles a 'six cord' thread which is the highest cord. The amount of twist and the number of cords gives the thread its character and each thread will produce a different type of lace.

Two cord threads are not tightly spun and bed down well to make a smooth flat type of lace. Three cord threads will have more twist and will form a firmer lace and four cord thread will make lace which is firmer still. Six cord thread is very smooth and round and except in its finer forms does not make good lace because the threads are too round to bed together.

Most linen threads are of two cord construction. Each reel will be marked with two numbers, for example, 60/2 or 90/3. This indicates the thickness of the thread and the number of cords. Some cottons are also marked by this system. It is possible to see the construction of a thread by untwisting a section at its cut end.

THE THREAD COUNT

The thread count is the thickness of the thread, which is often worked out from some ancient formula.

Linen thread is measured by the Lea System. It is based on yarn input. One lea represents a thread run of 300yd per pound. Sixty lea would have 18,000yd per pound and with the two cord system this would give 9,000yd per pound. A lea is sometimes called a hank, a rap or a cut. The higher the lea number, the finer the thread.

These measures are only approximate and do not take account of 'twist contraction' which reduces yardage by 10–15 per cent. To complicate matters, the Irish lace threads have their own system of numbering using numbers approximately 50 per cent larger than the lea number. For example, 100 lea 2-ply linen will have the number 150. This should be taken into consideration when choosing between Irish and continental linen threads. The continental threads, Bockens and Bouc use the Lea System without complications.

The following table indicates the Lea numbers used in continental threads with the comparable number from the Irish system. (The numbers are published by permission of Barbour Campbell Threads Ltd.)

LACE NUMBER	LINEN LEA NUMBER
30	25/2
40	30/2
50	35/2
60	40/2
70	45/2
80	50/2
100	60/2
150	100/2

The finest linen thread known had a count of 1,200, was produced in Flanders and dates from the seventeenth and eighteenth century. The finest machine-made linen thread available today has a count of 170 and the finest possible hand-spun thread probably has a count of 60.

Silk is measured by the denier system which is also used for man-made extruded fibres like nylon. A denier is the weight in grams of 9,000m. By this system the higher the number the thicker the thread.

The count of hand-spun wool varied from one part of the country to another. It could be the number of 200yd hanks per pound weight or the number of 320yd hanks per pound weight. However, we have long been used to the 2-py, 3-ply, 4-ply and double knitting system of purchasing wool and patterns to match.

Cotton has a count of the number of hanks or skeins of 840yd per pound weight. Cotton is manufactured with anything from two to six cords.

All these measures developed from the time of hand-spinning. They are a mixture of imperial and metric measurements. The great difficulty for the lacemaker is finding threads of comparable thickness across the whole range. If Cordonnet Special 100 is suitable, which would be the equivalent linen or silk?

As far back as 1873 an international

conference made an attempt to standardize all yarn in weight per length units. Progress was slow but finally, in 1962, the Tex System was agreed with the hope that it would be adopted world-wide. The Tex number of a yarn is the weight in grams of 1km (1,000m) of yarn.

For example, Tex 45 would mean that 1,000m of yarn weighed 45g. If the weight and length of a reel of thread are known, the Tex number can be worked out by the formula:

$$\frac{\text{Weight (grams)} \times 1000}{\text{Length (metres)}} = \text{Tex Number}$$

$$\frac{1\text{g} \times 1000}{18\text{m}} = \text{Tex 56}$$

Numbers are rounded to the nearest whole number. In this system the higher the number the thicker the thread.

Having thought that Tex numbers might be the answer, it has proved quite difficult to discover the numbers. With letters ignored or not answered directly I began to think that they were trade secrets. However, Madeira Threads (UK) Ltd started to publish the Tex numbers of their range and this proved a breakthrough as it acted as a lever to other companies. J. and C. Pipers provided me with the numbers of their silks and are now publishing them on their order forms. It is possible to work out the numbers from DMC threads because the weight and length is marked on the packs. Numbers supplied by them confirmed the correctness of the formula and of my arithmetic. Finally Barbour Campbell Threads Ltd gave me the numbers for linen threads.

The number of cords in the thread and the amount of twist affect thickness.

The following table gives the thread construction and Tex number of a variety of threads. The unbracketed numbers are published. The bracketed numbers are worked out using the formula. You will be able to slot other threads in at the appropriate level.

FIBRE	CONSTRUCTION	TEX
Wigley	180/2	6
Wigley	140/2	8
Wigley	120/2	10
Copley Marshall	120/2	10
Piper's Silk	210/2	10
Piper's Silk	140/2	14
Madeira Tanne	80/2	15
DMC Broder Machine (DMC Retors d'Alsace)	50/2	22
Piper's Silk	130/3	23
Madeira Tanne	50/2	24
Linen	Lea 100/2 (Irish 150)	33
DMC Broder Machine (DMC Retors d'Alsace)	30/2	37
Coats Supersheen	50/3	38
Madeira Tanne	30/2	40
Tootal Cotton	50/3	(40)
Piper's Silk	60/3	44
DMC Cordonnet Special	100/2/3	46
Linen	Lea 70/2 (Irish 110)	47
Coats Mercer Crochet	80/2/3	51
DMC Special Dentelles (DMC Fil à Dentelles)	70/80	(52)
Linen	Lea 60/2 (Irish 100)	55
Piper's Silk	50/3	61
Linen	Lea 50/2 (Irish 80)	66
DMC Coton Perle	12/2	(78)
Coats Mercer Crochet	40/2/3	90
Linen	35/2 (Irish 50)	95
Coats Mercer Crochet	30/2/3	102
DMC Coton Perle	8/2	(115)
DMC Coton Perle	5/2	(208)

3 Preparation

BOBBIN LACEMAKING

Bobbin lacemaking is a form of weaving. In traditional weaving, warp threads which run down the length of the fabric are fixed at both ends in a loom and various systems exist for lifting and lowering threads so that the weft thread can be passed back and forth between them to form a pattern.

In bobbin lace the threads are fixed to the pillow at the top of the work and the threads which are not in the working area are wound on bobbins which move through the work according to the pattern, and can become the warp or weft threads.

There is a limited number of ways in which threads can move over and under each other and all bobbin laces, no matter how simple or complex, use just two stitches, whole stitch and half stitch. Yet just as in knitting with its plain and purl, an infinite number of different designs can be produced.

TORCHON LACE

Torchon lace is easily identified by its combination of geometric shapes. Torchon is a French word variously translated as 'rag', 'dishcloth' and 'duster'. It derived from 'torcher', to wipe. In old French it meant twisted straw. By implication this is a coarse lace which will be useful for beginners to attempt as they will be able to see clearly what they are doing.

However, with growing expertise and the introduction of finer threads, a complex and very pretty lace can be produced.

Torchon lace was always a peasant lace, often called Beggar's Lace, Saxony Lace or Gueuse Lace and, although produced in Europe in the sixteenth and seventeenth centuries, was never a rival for the fine and beautiful laces favoured by the nobility. It originated in Saxony (northern Germany) and France and did not come to Britain until the end of the nineteenth century when it was made mostly in the East Midlands.

Torchon lace was used mainly in the form of narrow edgings and insertions to trim underwear. Heavier designs were used for household linens and soft furnishings. In Europe it had been made with bright-coloured threads but in this country it was usually white or ecru.

The use of a thick 'gimp' outlining thread was not traditional and first appears in Torchon designs from Sweden in the early twentieth century. Good copies of Torchon could be made on the Barmen machine. Fine Torchon was being made at Downton in Wiltshire, side by side with the traditional Downton designs, when the nationwide lace revival took place at the beginning of the twentieth century. To promote lacemaking the Old Downton Lace Industry was set up in 1910.

THE LACE DESIGN

Torchon lace is drafted on graph paper which comes in a variety of sizes. This makes it easy to vary the scale of the design and the thickness of the thread, according to the ultimate use of the lace. It is composed of a number of different motifs which can be put together in an infinite number of different designs. It will come as a series of dots on diagonal lines and areas which are plain. For a more comprehensive list of terms, *see* the Glossary on page 168.

Torchon Motifs

Diamonds   Diamond shapes of varying size; worked in a variety of ways.
Trails   Elongated diamonds which can be worked in whole or half stitch and can be worked on one angle, made to zigzag through the design or to form chevron shapes in the design.
Spiders   Motifs which fit a diamond shape in the pricking and can be constructed in a variety of ways.
Headsides   A variety of fan shapes in whole or half stitch or as a Torchon fan.
Triangles   Areas of whole stitch or half stitch with a horizontal or vertical straight edge.

Grounds for Torchon Lace

Each involves two pairs of bobbins and one pin-hole.

Torchon ground   Half stitch, pin, half stitch.
Dieppe ground   Half stitch, pin, half stitch and an extra twist on each pair.
Whole stitch ground   Whole stitch and twist, pin, whole stitch and twist.

Roseground   This ground involves four pairs of bobbins and four pin-holes. It is described in Pattern 6.
Honeycomb ground   A ground more often found in Bucks point lace but sometimes used in Torchon. It is worked in two alternate rows and is described in Pattern 12.

The beginner may have the design supplied by the teacher or may trace or photocopy a design from a book. Photocopying is frowned upon by the traditionalists who feel that every pattern should be drafted by the lacemaker. However, this is time-consuming and not easy for a beginner anxious to make lace. Photocopying causes some distortion but tracing, if not accurate, can cause even more. To make good lace you must have an accurate design which is accurately pricked.

In the past, rubbings were taken. This involved placing tracing paper on the back of an existing pricking (with the owner's permission) and sweeping a stick of heelball[1] across it in the manner of brass rubbing. This copied the back of a pricking so the tracing paper could be turned over, placed on card and pricked in the normal manner. It is unwise to prick through one pricking to form another as this can cause damage to the original.

MAKING A PRICKING IN THE TRADITIONAL MANNER

The lace pattern, pricking or parchment should be made of pricking card which is made specifically for the purpose and comes in a buff colour with a glazed

[1]Mixture of hard wax and lampblack

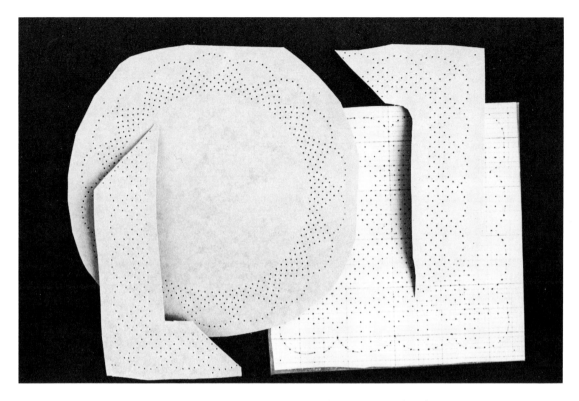

Two types of prickings. Left, glazed pricking card; right, photocopy, card and transparent film 'sandwich'.

surface. An alternative is good quality card from some breakfast cereal packets or card from packets of tights.

Place the design on the card and fix with paper clips. Pin both layers to a pricking board. This can be a cork mat or a piece of polystyrene, even the underside of a polystyrene pillow. Do not be tempted to use the top of the pillow. You want to preserve this surface for making lace. (Advice on prickers can be found in Chapter 1 on Equipment.)

Hold the pricker vertically, and systematically prick through all the dots on the draft as accurately as possible. When you think you have completed the pricking remove the card and draft from the base and hold it up to the light or look at the reverse side. Any holes unpricked can be easily seen. Transfer any necessary

markings to the pricking, first in pencil and then in permanent ink.

An alternative way to make a pricking would be to fix a photocopy to some card and cover with coloured transparent book film to make a three-layer sandwich which can be pricked. Any pattern markings will show clearly through the book film. Book film comes in a variety of colours and with a matt or shiny surface. The colours provide a good contrast with white thread though only experience will tell which colour is best. I like matt blue, which is more expensive and less easily available than shiny yellow or orange. I find shiny green and blue very difficult but have students who manage very well with it. It is necessary to cover a photocopy because the friction of the thread's on the print will soil the work.

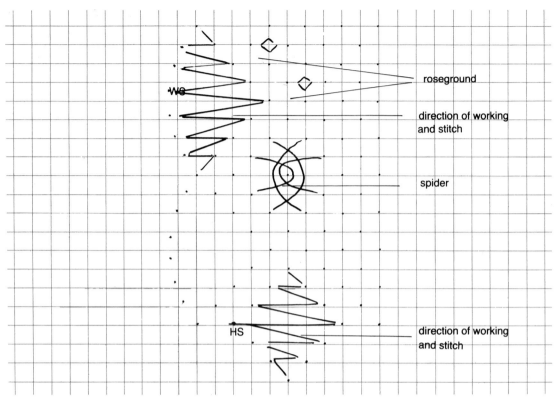

roseground

direction of working and stitch

spider

direction of working and stitch

HS

WS

Pattern markings.

PATTERN MARKINGS

Dressing the Pillow

When the pricking is completed it must be pinned to the pillow at each corner, with pins that are pushed in until they are flush with the pricking.

If a mushroom pillow is being used the top of the pricking should be at the top of the slope or just over. This way the maximum length can be worked with the bobbins resting on the pillow, without the necessity of moving the lace.

Square and round motifs should be placed in the middle of the pillow. Use a cover cloth pinned firmly and horizontally across the pillow and pricking, exposing the top 2in (5cm) of the pricking. Place the pins at the edges of the pillow flush with the cloth. As work progresses

this cloth will be moved down the pillow to expose more of the pricking. A pincushion can be placed to right or left depending on which feels most convenient. This is called 'dressing the pillow'.

WINDING BOBBINS

Bobbins are wound in pairs with a continuous piece of thread for the beginning of a new piece of lace. No knots are allowed in lace. The length of thread needed comes with experience and there is advice given in the first pattern (*see* page 46).

Make sure your hands and work surface are clean, and handle the thread as little as possible. The thread should pass around the bobbin in a clockwise direction. I find it is best to hold the bobbin in

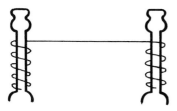

Winding bobbins.

the left hand, make a couple of turns of thread round the bobbin so that the end is held firmly and then to turn the bobbin along the length of the thread. Winding round a stationary bobbin sometimes results in the thread plies becoming untwisted as the lace is being made. Wind the second bobbin in the same way. Wind so that the bobbins are within 8in (20cm) of each other and place a hitch round the top of the bobbin to secure the thread. If the total length of thread is only one arm's length, one bobbin can be attached to each end and then the pair wound towards each other, making sure both are being turned clockwise.

If pairs are not to be used immediately they should be stored separately in a bobbin bag or on a bobbin tree; threads become knotted very easily. A bobbin

winder can be used to save time especially if a large number of pairs with a large amount of thread are necessary.

ARE YOU SITTING COMFORTABLY?

It is most important that you sit comfortably in a good light when making lace, otherwise you will have an aching back and eye-strain.

I am tall and find I can work comfortably in an armchair with the pillow on my knees. You may find it more comfortable to sit with the whole pillow resting on a table, possibly propped at an angle, or with the top edge of the pillow resting on a table and the bottom edge on your knee. Modern pillow stands with adjustable height can be made or purchased, sometimes with a light incorporated in the design.

Good daylight is the best working light. Sit near a window if the sky is grey. Strong electric light, possibly from an adjustable angled lamp can be used after dark. Daylight bulbs are becoming more readily available but they are expensive and the light they give may be too hard for some people.

In the past the pillow was rested on a stand called a 'horse' or a 'maid'. These stands were made by local carpenters,

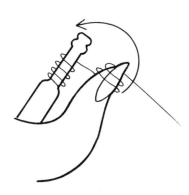

Putting a hitch on a bobbin.

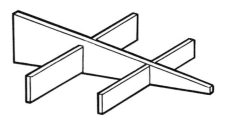

A table rest.

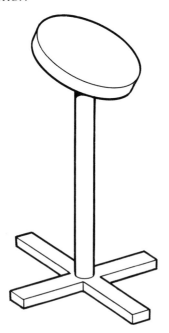

A modern free-standing pillow rest.

A flash stool.

wheelwrights or coopers in a variety of designs. The two main types were the single horse or the bowed horse. Each had a tripod of legs. The single horse was topped with a bar on which the pillow was propped while resting on the work-

A 'horse' or 'maid'.

er's knees. The bowed horse had a half-hoop bow attached to the bar. The whole pillow could rest on this bow without any other support.

Lacemakers worked out of doors whenever possible. In bad weather and in the dark days of winter they worked by candle-light. To make the best of the candle-light a flash stool was used. This was a three-legged stool, about 2ft (50cm) high, with a series of holes in the top. A central hole held the candle, which could be raised as it burned down. Around the edge were three, four or five similar holes. These were used to hold flashes or flasks of 'snow water'. These flashes worked in the same way as lenses and concentrated the light on the work in progress. The lacemakers could sit in a circle and make the most of one candle. When in use, the flashes rested on a flash cushion, an open circle of plaited rushes. When not in use they rested in hutches, which were small rush baskets hung on the stool.

4   Making Lace

Patterns 1–12 are designed to introduce most of the motifs and techniques of Torchon lace in a series of simple insertions edgings and mats. I do not like scrappy samples which is why I appear to be so fond of bookmarks and small mats!

For a beginner, lacemaking is a slow process, so small is beautiful. The patterns are drafted on graph paper with 10 squares to 25mm and the samples worked with Cordonnet Special 100. (DMC Retors d'Alsace 30, sewing cotton or an equivalent thread could be used.) Before beginning each pattern, study the pricking, photograph and working diagram. Try to trace the paths of the threads and understand what you are doing.

The photographs of the samples are taken from the wrong side, which is facing up. The right side of the lace is to the pillow. Complete pieces are photographed from the right side unless otherwise stated.

PATTERN 1
STITCH SAMPLE

6 pairs bobbins with approx ¾yd (0.75m) thread on each bobbin.

1.   Make the pricking.
2.   Dress the pillow.
3.   Wind six pairs of bobbins.
4.   Place pins at a, b, c, d, e and f. Pins should slope slightly backwards and feel firm in their positions, with about ⅓ of their lengths in the pillow. Edge pins should slope slightly outwards to stop the lace rising up and distorting the final shape.
5.   Hang one pair on each of the pins at a, b, c, d, e and f.
6.   You are going to take the pair from f over to g. These threads will be called the 'weavers'. The pairs from a, b, c, d and e will be called the 'passives'.
7*.   Take the pair from f and the pair from a and number their positions 1, 2, 3, 4.
8.   Using your left hand lift the bobbin at position 2 over position 3.
9.   Using both hands lift the bobbin now at 2 over 1 and position 4 over 3.
10.   Using your left hand lift the bobbin now at position 2 over position 3**. This is one whole stitch and the four threads are now intertwined over and under each other as in weaving and darning.
11.   Push the left-hand pair aside and take the right-hand pair, which has come from f and the pair from b and work * to **.
12.   Push the left-hand pair aside and take the weavers from f through pairs from c, d and e in the same manner.
13.   Twist the weavers twice, the right-hand bobbin over the left. Put up pin g to the right of the pair from e and under the weavers. Pull the weavers taut and straighten the passives, to give good tension.

> **Check**
> •   The same two threads run across from f to g.
> •   There are no twists on the passives.

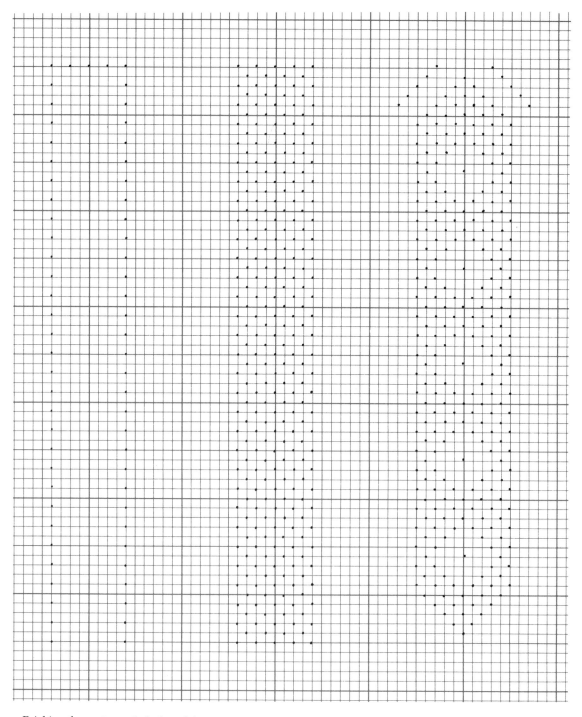

Pricking for patterns 1, 2, 3 and 4.

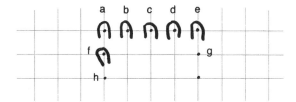

Setting up pattern 1.

14. Using exactly the same motions, take the pair from g back to h using * to **. Just remember you are working towards the left and worked passives will be pushed to the right. *Do not* be tempted to reverse the stitch.

15. Twist the weavers twice, right over left, and put up pin h to the left of the passives from a and under the weavers.

> **Check**
> • You now have four threads across the pillow intertwined with ten passives.
> • You are twisting the weavers twice right over left before placing the pin at the end of each row. Without the twists you have two untidy loops when the pin is removed.
> • Tension. Good tension comes with practice. The thread is surprisingly strong and you are aiming to produce an area with the appearance of cloth.

16. When you feel confident with whole stitch, change to half stitch.

17. Start with the weavers at a left-hand pin. Take the weavers and first passives and number positions 1, 2, 3, 4. *Take 2 over 3 and simultaneously 2 over 1 and 4 over 3**. This is a half stitch.

18. Push the left-hand pair aside and take the weavers through the next pair to the right * to **. Work all the pairs to the right-hand edge.

19. In half stitch the weavers will already have one twist on them, so make

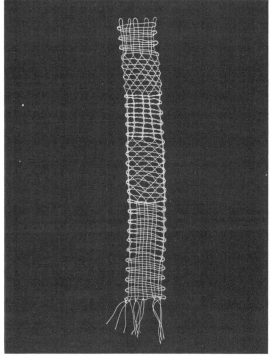

Pattern 1. A stitch sample.

one more twist, right over left before placing the pin between the weavers and the last passive pair worked.

> **Check**
> • You have brought one thread across the work but you still have two threads going round the pin and all the passives are crossed, the left-hand thread of each pair above the right.

20. Work towards the left in exactly the same manner. You are now producing a stitch with a lattice pattern.

21. As you work, check that the weavers are taken through pairs in which the left-hand thread is above the right and has neither an extra twist nor becomes

untwisted. The single thread which works backwards and forwards across the work is from the same bobbin.

Check
- As a patch of half stitch develops, you will find that the right-hand thread of each pair runs diagonally from the left-hand edge of the work. The left-hand thread runs diagonally from the right-hand edge and the weaver is forming horizontal lines.
- Because the threads go in three different directions it is easier to get good tension in half stitch. However, beginners are sometimes frightened by it, because it is easy to lose your way if you are distracted.

Advice
- If you have to leave the work, perhaps because the phone rings, use coloured headed pins or some memory jogger to mark your working position.
- If you get lost, unpick to the last pin placed and sort out the pairs.

---

22. When you feel confident in whole stitch and half stitch, try whole stitch and twist.
23. Start after placing a pin. Work 2 over 3, 2 over 1 and 4 over 3 simultaneously, 2 over 3, 2 over 1 and 4 over 3 simultaneously. This is two half stitches one on top of the other and if worked across all the pairs has the effect of spacing the weavers and passives and forming a chequered pattern.
24. A half stitch on a headside fan does not hold its shape well. It is best used with a whole stitch and twist worked before and after the edge pin. Try working whole stitch and twist before and after the edge pins and half stitch through the three centre pairs of the strip.

25. Try whole stitch and twist before and after the edge pins and whole stitch through the three centre pairs.
26. You have tried all the stitches used in lacemaking. Lace is made of a combination of these stitches. Your aim is to know and to work them automatically.
27. Try various combinations of stitches until the pricking is complete.
28. Finish with the weavers at the edge. Place the pin and make a reef knot (left thread over right and right over left), one of the weavers with each of the edge stitch pair. Tie the other pairs together with reef knots.
29. Cut off bobbins and carefully remove pins. Do not remove pins before cutting off bobbins. The weight of the bobbins will distort your lace if it is not supported by pins.

A reef knot.

How Much Thread on Each Bobbin?

It is best to try and make the complete piece of lace without adding new thread. It is always difficult to know how much thread to put on the bobbins. It depends on the motifs in the pricking.

My suggestions are very approximate. I do not use a tape measure. I know the extent of my arms is about 60in (1.5m) (the length of the tape) and how to measure an approximate yard or metre and so on.

Advice
- Weavers in a whole stitch fan need a great deal of thread because they work backward and forward through all the fans on an edging.
- Passives in a fan on the other hand pass round the edge of the lace in an almost straight line though some length is taken up in the weaving.
- Ground pairs work diagonally backwards and forwards but will sometimes become weavers in diamonds etc. and this uses extra threads.
- One footside pair remains constant, the others go in and out of the ground.
- Whatever happens, no knots should be worked in the lace. If you are running short of thread on a particular bobbin you can manipulate to a certain extent.
- If you are working on an area of half stitch, put an extra twist on the weaver pair after placing the pin. This will send a different bobbin across the work.
- At the top of a diamond or chevron examine both pairs. Either pair can become the weavers. Just work to the left instead of the right as instructed in the diamond bookmark (*see* page 51).
- If a fan weaver pair is running short of thread, work the edge stitch and cover the pin. Now swap the pairs by lifting the weavers up and passing the edge pair underneath. The weavers will become the edge pair and the edge pair will become the weavers. New thread can then be added at the edge as described below. This manoeuvre is necessary because a double thread as weaver will thicken up the fan. Double threads on passives are less obvious.
- If you think there may be enough thread to complete the work but it will not stay attached to the bobbin, attach it to a newly wound single bobbin with a weaver knot. Using the new bobbin, make a

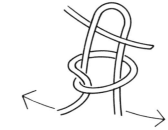

A weaver knot.

loop as at the start of knitting. Put the short end through the loop and pull the loop shut. With luck the end will become part of the knot. If not, try again. Trim the ends and continue work. The knot must not go into the work. If this looks likely, wind a new single bobbin and tie it to a pin at the side of the work. Bring the thread through the work and down beside the bobbin to be replaced. Tie both bobbins together with a freezer bag closure, elastic band or some device of your own and work both bobbins as one for a short spell until the new thread is secure in the work. Untie the pair and put the knotted bobbin to the back of the work, over the pins. When you are sure that no mistakes have been made in this area of work this bobbin can be cut off. The thread end can be cut off close to the work when the whole piece is complete. If in doubt sew the end in. Do not remove the pin holding the new bobbin at the side until a considerable amount of lace has been worked. If the end is released you could find it pulling right through the work.
- Broken threads. If you have the misfortune to break a thread, unpick your work until a short end of thread is available. Attach it to a newly wound single bobbin by a weaver's knot as previously described. Join in a new parallel thread and throw back the broken thread before the knot is reached.
- Advice on unpicking. It is frequently necessary to unpick lace to correct mistakes or as mentioned to repair a broken thread. Lacemakers become adept at unpicking and all will go well if pins are left in position until they are released from the threads. Always unpick systematically right back to a pin before removing it from the pricking. To do otherwise is to achieve a muddle that may never be sorted.

PATTERN 2 TORCHON GROUND AND FOOTSIDE

12 pairs bobbins with approx 1yd (1m) thread on each bobbin.

Two of these pairs could be wound with coloured sewing cotton or crochet cotton. I added pink pairs of slightly thicker thread which do not show in the photograph except in what appears to be a very crooked footside (the straight edge).

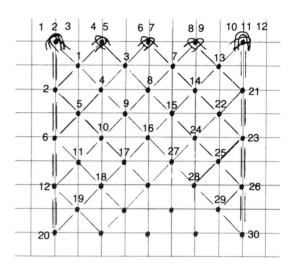

Working Torchon ground and footside.

Advice

Having learned the stitches in lace we will now put them to use in an insertion of Torchon ground and footside.

- Torchon ground is worked down the diagonal lines of the pricking, always starting with the hole furthest away from you. The lines can be worked either from top right to bottom left or top left to bottom right, using the pairs which cross each other naturally at the pin-holes.
- As work progresses you will see that each pin down the diagonal has a pair hanging from it. If you have worked the line correctly you should have three pairs left to work the footside hole at the end of each row. If two coloured pairs are used the path of individual threads can be seen more clearly.

The Ground

1. Make the pricking. Mark in some of the diagonal lines at the beginning of the pricking. As you work the lines should become covered with thread.
2. Dress the pillow.
3. Wind twelve pairs of bobbins.
4. Hang three pairs on the two outer holes and two pairs on each of the three inner holes. Hang the coloured threads at positions 6 and 7.
5. Take the third and fourth pairs from the left and make a half stitch. Place a pin

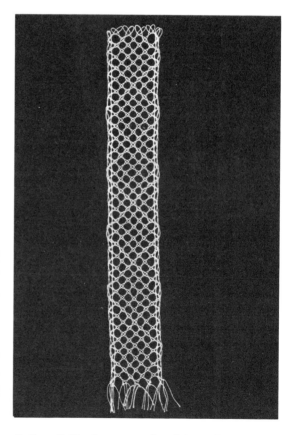

Pattern 2. Torchon ground and footside.

between the pairs at 1. Cover the pin with a half stitch.
6. Use left-hand pair from 1 and first and second pairs from left to make a footside at 2.

The Footside

Take third and second pair from outer edge and work whole stitch and twist.

Take second and first pair from edge and work whole stitch and twist. Put an extra twist on the first (outermost) pair. Place pin inside two pairs, that is between second and third pair from outer edge. Ignore first (outermost) pair and use second and third pairs to cover pin with whole stitch and twist. This is the sequence for a Torchon footside and is worked in the same manner for both the left-hand and right-hand edge.

7. Take fifth and sixth pairs from left and make a half stitch. Place a pin between them at 3. Cover the pin with a half stitch.
8. Working diagonally down the line, use left-hand pair from 3 and right-hand pair from 1 to half stitch, pin, half stitch at 4.
9. Take left-hand pair from 4 and innermost pair from 2 to make 5.
10. Take left-hand pair from 5 and two pairs from 2 for footside at 6. One of the coloured pairs should have made the diagonal line.
11. Take seventh and eighth pairs from the left to make 7.
12. Work diagonally as before through 8, 9, 10, 11, in half stitch, pin, half stitch and work 12 as a footside.
13. Take ninth and tenth pairs for 13 and down the line to a footside at 20.
14. Now try using the opposite diagonal. Use right-hand pair from 13 and the

last two unused pairs on the right to make a footside at 21.
15. Use the inner pair from 21 and the right-hand pair from 14 for 22.
16. Use the right-hand pair from 22 and the last two pairs on right for a footside at 23. The coloured pair should have made this diagonal through pins 7, 14, 22 and 23.
17. The right-hand pair from 15 and the left-hand pair from 22 for 24 etc.
18. Continue in like manner, working diagonally in one direction or the other until the pricking is complete.
19. Tie each pair of bobbins with a reef knot. Cut off bobbins and carefully remove pins.
20. Admire your first piece of lace!
21. The wrong side of the lace is facing you. The right side is against the pillow.

Abbreviations
Having worked two samples with every move spelt out it now seems sensible to use some abbreviations to save time and space. Continue to use the techniques already learned.

prs	pairs	**LH**	left hand
L	left	**WS**	whole stitch
R	right	**HS**	half stitch
RH	right hand		

The next sample will make a bookmark starting and ending in a point. It could, however, be extended to make a belt or a decoration for household linen, or an idea of your own.

Calculating the Number of Pairs you will Need
This is usually done by counting down a complete diagonal line and adding one pair. Extra pairs will then be needed according to the form of the lace, one extra pair for each footside, three or four extra pairs for a fan. In this pattern one extra pair will be needed for each footside. This makes a total of fourteen pairs.

PATTERN 3
DIAMOND STRIP

14 prs bobbins with approx 1yd (1m) thread on each bobbin.

1. Make a pricking and study it.
2. Dress the pillow. When starting at a point, pairs are hung on support pins – in this case pins a to j. After the pins in the prickings have been worked the support pins are removed and the loops will drop down to form a neat beginning.
3. Hang two prs on 1. Twist RH pr twice. Work WS and twist to cover the pin.
4. Hang one pr on a and use it with RH pr from 1 to work HS pin HS at 2.
5. Work HS pin HS with prs on b, c and d for pins 3, 4 and 5.

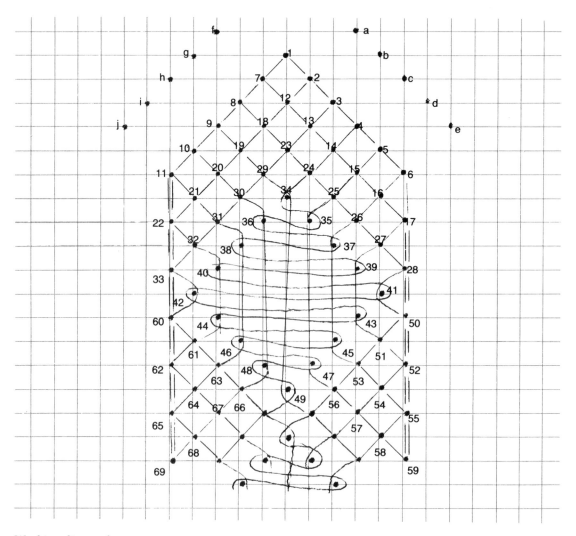

Working diamonds.

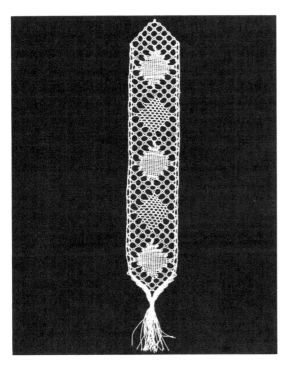

Pattern 3. A diamond strip (whole and half stitch diamonds with half stitch ground).

6. Two prs at e and RH pr from 5 will make a footside at 6.

7. Remove pins at a, b, c, d and e and allow threads to fall to 2, 3, 4, 5 and 6.

8. Hang prs on f, g, h, i and j and work pins 7, 8, 9, 10 and 11 in similar fashion. 11 will be a footside. Remove pins at f, g, h, i and j.

9. Work HS pin HS at 12 with prs from 7 and 2.

10. HS pin HS at 13 with prs from 12 and 3.

11. Continue down the diagonal through 14, 15 and 16 in HS pin HS.

12. At 17 work footside with 3 prs.

13. At 18, 19, 20 and 21 work HS pin HS.

14. At 22 work footside.

15. Work 23 to 27 in HS pin HS and 28 as footside.

16. Work 29 to 32 in HS pin HS and 33 as footside.

17. The next row of holes form the top of the diamond and are needed in its working.

The Diamond

1. Take prs from 29 and 24 and work WS. Twist LH pr twice. Place pin at 34. The LH pair will become the weavers and will work the passives in WS.

2. Cover pin with WS and continue to right through pr from 25. Twist weavers twice and place pin 35.

3. Work to left in WS through 2 pairs and work through new pr from 30. Twist weavers and place pin 36.

4. Work to right through 3 prs and through new pr from 26. Twist weavers and place pin 37.

5. Work to L through 4 prs and bring in new pr from 31. Twist and place 38.

6. Work to R through 5 prs and bring in new pr from 27. Twist and place 39.

7. Work to L through 6 prs and bring in new pr from 32. Twist and place 40.

8. R through 7 prs and new pr from 28. Twist and place 41.

9. L through 8 prs and new pr from 33. Twist and place 42.

Check
One pair has been taken in diagonally from the ground at each of the pin-holes from 34 to 42. The diamond is now at its widest and pairs will start being left out after each pin so that they can re-enter the diagonal ground lines.

---

10. Work R through 8 prs leaving 1 pr against 41. Twist and place 43.

11. Work L through 7 prs leaving 1 pr against 42. Twist and place 44.
12. Work R through 6 prs leaving 1 pr against 43. Twist and place 45.
13. Work L through 5 prs leaving 1 pr against 44. Twist and place 46.
14. Work R through 4 prs leaving 1 pr against 45. Twist and place 47.
15. Work L through 3 prs leaving 1 pr against 46. Twist and place 48.
16. Work R through 2 prs leaving 1 pr against 47. Twist and place 49.
17. Cover 49 with WS and twist.
18. Put twist on all pairs 41 to 49.

Check

If the diamond has been worked correctly there will be two pairs left to work the final hole.

A pin can be placed at each side of the pillow and the pairs left against the pins down the diamond can be placed behind them as a reminder that you have worked through sufficient pairs before placing the next pin.

Return to Ground Stitches

1. Work 50 as footside with prs from 41 and edge.
2. Work 51 with prs from 43 and 50.
3. Work 52 as footside. Continue in sequence to 59, move to the left side and work 60 to 69 in like manner. Complete one more row of ground and footside on each side of the diamond before starting the next diamond.
4. When you feel confident about whole stitch diamonds, you can try one in half stitch.
5. Work as far as the bottom 'V' of holes.

Finishing a Bookmark at a Point

1. Work as far as the bottom 'V' of holes.
2. Take pr from l and work WS to edge. Twist weavers twice and put up pin a.
3. Work back through 2 passive prs in WS and leave among the passives.
4. Take pr from m and work WS to edge. Twist weavers twice, put up pin b and work back through 2 pairs and leave.
5. Continue in like manner placing pins c, d and e. After e take weavers through all prs and leave on inside of group.
6. Work pins f to j in like manner.
7. Work k, WS pin WS using weavers from each bundle.
8. Reef knot both pairs to secure stitch. Pull all pairs to produce a good tension.
9. Cut off the bobbins leaving about 2in (5cm) of thread to form a plait at the bottom of the bookmark. Divide the threads into three bundles and make a neat plait. Secure the end with a knotted thread.

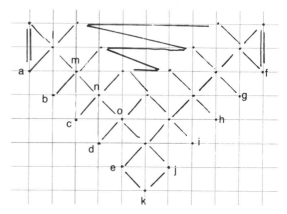

Finishing a bookmark.

PATTERN 4
SPIDER BOOKMARK

14 prs bobbins with approx 1yd (1m) thread on each bobbin.

The pricking made for the diamond bookmark can be used for this piece of lace. The number of bobbins and quantity of thread required will be the same. The Torchon ground has been replaced by a whole stitch and twist ground.

1. Dress the pillow.
2. Follow the directions for setting up the diamond bookmark in Pattern 3 but work WS and twist instead of HS.
3. Work WS and twist ground and footsides down diagonal lines until all the holes including those around the top of the diamond are filled.

To Make a Spider

4. Twist the pairs from 1, 2, 3, 4, 5 and 6 three times.

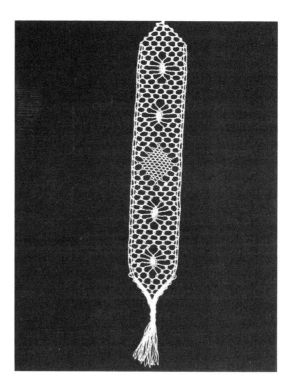

Pattern 4. A spider bookmark (spiders and half stitch diamond with whole stitch ground).

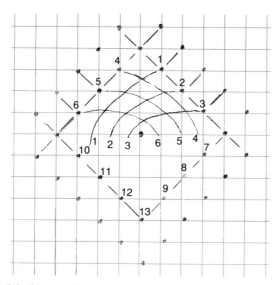

Working spiders.

5. Spiders are worked in whole stitch.
6. Take pr from 4 and work WS through prs from 1, 2 and 3.
7. Take pr from 5 and work WS through prs from 1, 2 and 3.
8. Take pr from 6 and work WS through prs from 1, 2 and 3.
9. You have passed three prs through three prs.
10. Place pin in centre of diamond with three pairs on either side of it. Tension the threads.
11. Take 3 through 6, 5 and 4.
12. Take 2 through 6, 5 and 4.
13. Take 1 through 6, 5 and 4.
14. Three prs have again passed through three prs. Tension the threads.
15. Twist each pair three times.

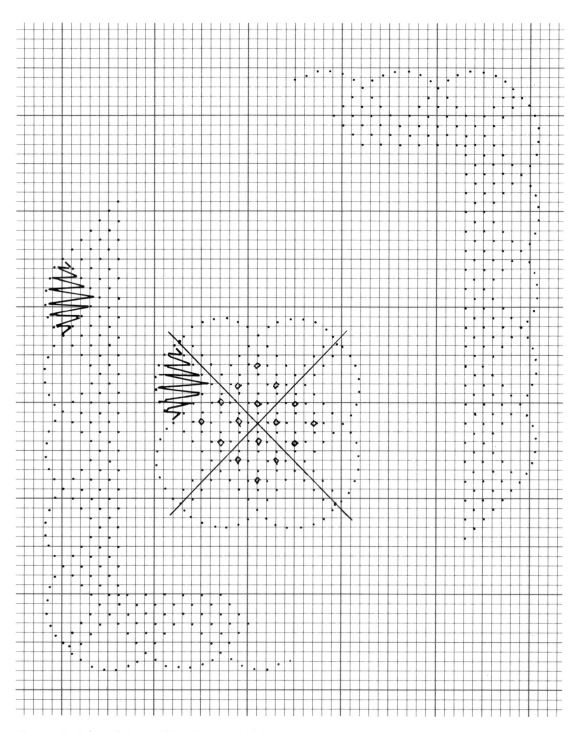

Pattern 5. A fan edging pricking. Pattern 6. A fan and roseground pricking.

16.   On right, work appropriate prs into 7, 8 and 9 using WS twist pin WS twist.
17.   On left, work appropriate prs into 10, 11 and 12 using WS twist pin WS twist.
18.   Use prs from 12 and 9 to work 13.
19.   This is the simplest Torchon spider. It can vary in size from two to as many as six 'legs' in each side. The number of twist placed on the 'legs' can be varied according to the size of the spider and the thickness of the thread.
20.   Continue the bookmark by working the next area of ground stitches followed by further spiders.
21.   Complete the bookmark as described for the diamond bookmark.

Variations

As with the diamond bookmark this pricking can be extended for some other use. Diamonds can alternate with spiders. Half stitch Torchon ground can be used.

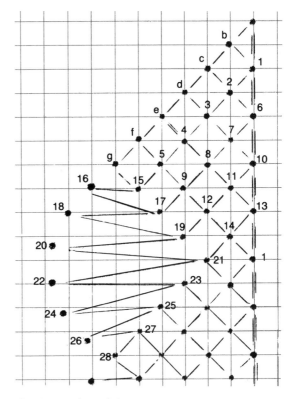

Setting up fan edging.

PATTERN 5
FAN EDGING

11 prs bobbins with 1yd (1m) on each weaver pair and ½yd (0.5m) on all other bobbins.

1.   Make pricking of one straight section and dress the pillow.
2.   Hang two prs on 1 and one pr on b, c, d, e and f.
3.   Using prs at 1, twist RH bobbins three times. WS and twist to cover pin.
4.   Discard RH pr. Take LH pr and pr from b and work WS and twist. Do not put up a pin.
5.   Discard RH pr. Take LH pr and pr from c and work HS pin HS at 2.

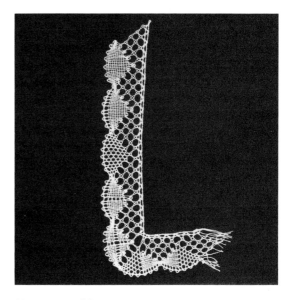

Variations of fans.

6. Discard RH pr and with LH pr and pr from d work HS pin HS at 3.
7. Work 4 and 5 with prs from e and f.
8. Carefully remove support pins b, c, d, e and f and pull down loops.
9. Place all pins to 14, working footsides at 6, 10, 13, and HS pin HS at other holes.

The Fan

1. Hang four prs on g in order, right to left. The LH pr will be the weavers. The other three prs must be used to fill the curved area of the fan. The inner edge of the fan is one side of a diamond and is worked in the way already practised.
2. Using LH pr as weaver, work WS to right through three prs on g and pr hanging from 5. Twist weavers twice and place pin 15.
3. Work to left through all prs in WS. Twist weavers twice and place pin 16.
4. Continue to 28, taking in at 17, 19 and 21 and leaving out at 21, 23 etc.
5. At 28 leave weavers at outside. Push them and three fan prs to left.
6. Return to right-hand side and starting with footside 1 work as before.

Variations of the Fan

1. All WS.
2. All WS with WS and twist before and after edge pins 16, 18, 20 etc. Twist weavers once before working edge pair and placing pin.
3. HS, with WS and twist before and after edge pins.
4. After 21 has been put up, twist the passive prs once each and continue in the usual way. This is a WS and twist fan edge.
5. Again in a WS fan, twist weavers in same position in each row. Different

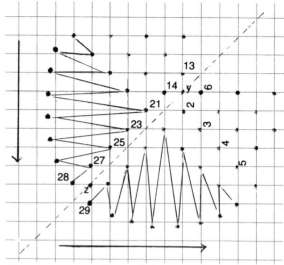

Turning corner of fans edging.

numbers of twists give different effects.
6. and 7. Worked partly in half stitch and partly in whole stitch.

The Corner

1. Complete the diagonal 13, 14, 21, 23, 25, 27 and 28.
2. Work y as a footside.
3. Work z by taking the weavers at 28 to the right through the three fan prs.
4. Place pin z and work back to left through three prs. Place 29 at beginning of new fan. This sequence has brought the weavers to the normal outside position for starting a new fan.
5. Turn the pillow to bring the new fan to the normal position.
6. Work fan as usual. Use pr from fan and pr from y to work 2. The three remaining prs will work 6.

Colour

Coloured thread can be used in the fan edge. It works best in one of the whole stitch variations. Too great a contrast will highlight uneven working, but the colour chosen will appear paler in the work than on the reel. Experience will tell.

All the pairs hung at the top of the fan at g may be coloured, or the colour can be confined to the weaver pair, the left-hand pair placed last on the pin.

Round Mat Using Fan Edging

12 prs bobbins with plenty of thread on the weaver pr.

1.   By following the instructions for the fan edging, a round mat can be worked. As the ground area is wider, an extra pair of bobbins is required.

2.   Centre the pricking on the middle of a mushroom pillow. Decide which variation of fan or fans you are going to use.
3.   As work progresses around the mat it will be necessary to push pins in flush with the pricking. Push in all pins on the first repeat and all round if you have sufficient pins. Otherwise leave them in on both edges and carefully remove others to use as the work progresses.
4.   If you have used coloured threads in the footside and ground pattern you will have seen the path which threads take through the ground. This path can easily act as a gathering thread if insufficient pins are left in the work, especially immediately behind the working area.
5.   As you near the end of the circle, a piece of clear plastic over the pins at the

Unmounted round and square mats using fan edging.

A round fan edging mat.

beginning of the work will allow you to see the work without catching thread on the pins.

6. When the whole pricking has been worked the edges must be joined by means of sewings.

Sewings

1. Pairs are sewn into the hole which would naturally be worked with that pair.
2. Work the lace as far as possible.
3. If not already done, pin the beginning of the lace in its correct position on the pricking and for about 1in (2.5cm) back.
4. Check which pairs should work which holes.
5. Remove one pin and place a fine crochet hook or latchet hook through the hole.
6. Catch up the LH thread of the

appropriate pair and bring it through the hole to form a loop.
7. Pass the other bobbin of the pair through the loop and pull both bobbins gently to close the loop and correct the tension.
8. Replace the pin and move to the next hole.
9. For fans and footside holes more than one pair will need to be brought through the hole. This can be done with care.
10. I usually start in the middle of the edging and work systematically towards both edges.
11. When all sewings are completed into the correct holes, knot each pair R over L, L over R and R over L, as in a reef knot with an extra half knot.
12. The bobbins can be cut off close to the work but for extra insurance, especially if the lace is to be laundered, bob-

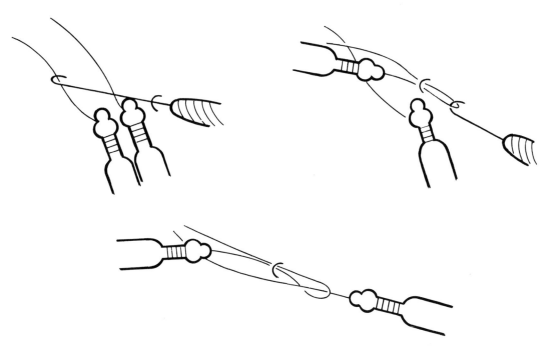

Making a join with sewings.

bins can be cut off leaving 2in (5cm) ends of thread. These can be individually threaded into a fine needle and woven through the lace in the same direction as the worked lace for about ½in (13mm). Take one thread from each pair in opposite directions. Trim the ends close to the lace.

13.   Pairs from the fan can be oversewn in a tight bundle to the underside of a fan, using one thread for sewing and gradually dropping pairs out of the bundle to graduate the thickness of the bundle down to nothing.

14.   Now mount the lace on a suitable fabric. Advice is given in Chapter 5.

15.   If the lace is to be mounted in a frame or under a paperweight some or all of the ends left after the sewings can be threaded through the fabric backing and tied and trimmed on the wrong side. Beware of the thread ends showing through if the backing fabric is fine.

Magic Loop

Sewings which require more than one pair to be pulled through can be made easier by insertion of a magic loop when the lace is set up.

Take a pair of bobbins and knot them together with about 6in (15cm) coloured thread. Hang them on a pin at the side of the pricking. Bring the pair to the right of pin g and pass them between all the pairs on pin g and out to the left-hand side of the work.

When it is time to make the sewing, bobbins can be passed through the magic loop, the pin at g can be removed and the coloured thread gently pulled. It should pass out of the hole and bring the bobbin threads with it. Sewings can then be completed in the normal way.

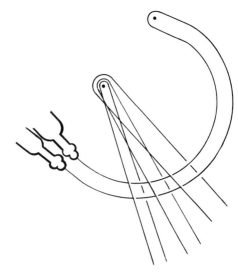

A magic loop.

When you understand the process, the loop can be placed in position without being attached to bobbins. If you have the patience you can place coloured loops at all the setting up pins and this should speed up making the sewings.

Using a Lazy Susan and Bent Needle Pin

These two implements use the same principle to make sewings.

1.   Place a piece of coloured thread about 6in (15cm) long through the eye of the needle.

2.   Push the eye and thread through the pin-hole in the lace.

3.   Pull the thread away from the eye of the needle to form a loop.

4.   Place the left-hand bobbin through the loop.

5.   Withdraw the needle and cotton from the hole and the bobbin thread should come with it to form a loop.

6. Place the other bobbin through this loop and complete the sewing as before.

Square Mat using Fan Edging

The patterns worked so far have fitted a mushroom pillow and it has been necessary to move the lace during working.

If a mushroom pillow is being used and a large square or long length of lace is required it may be necessary to move the lace up the pillow or turn the lace and pricking at a corner. Make a lifting pad.

1. Make both sections of pricking and cut the card carefully so that the edges will match and the holes will properly align. Each section will be worked twice in rotation to form the complete square.
2. Decide which type of fan or fans you will use.
3. Dress the pillow with one pricking section.
4. Set up and begin working the lace as instructed but at the beginning of the second repeat. This will make joining easier. The sewings will not be made over a join in the pricking.
5. Work three repeats of the pattern. Unpin the end of the pricking and slide the lifting pad underneath, as close to the lace as possible. Re-pin the pricking firmly over the pad.
6. Continue working up on to the pad until there are plenty of pins in the highest area.
7. Unpin the cover cloth and use it to make a tight bundle around the bobbin. Pin the cloth several times to make it secure.
8. Remove all pins which go directly into the pillow.

9. Support the bobbin bundle and ease the lifting pad off the pillow.
10. Reposition the pad further up the pillow so that you can work the next section of pattern in comfort.
11. Push the pins in the pad through to the pillow so that the lace is secure.
12. Replace some of the pins in the lace beyond the pad so that the threads do not pull through.
13. Unpin the cover cloth, sort the bobbins and continue work.
14. Pin the new section of pricking to the pillow, being careful to align it correctly.
15. Carry on working until the lifting pad is necessary again.
16. Do not try to move the lace and add a section of pricking at the same time. New sections should be joined on the pillow and never on the lifting pad.
17. Keep plenty of pins in the lace to prevent threads pulling through and gathering the work.
18. Work each section twice and then the first repeat of the first section to make a complete square.
19. Repin the first repeat of the lace in its correct position, making very sure that there are no twists in the edging, before making the sewings. Now mount the lace on a suitable fabric. Advice is given in Chapter 5.
20. If you wish to make a larger square or an oblong shape, make a pricking of extra repeats of the pattern as necessary.
21. Long straight lengths of this or any other edging can be made by making two sections of pricking which match each other when moved in sequence.
22. The pricking can be moved up the pillow as necessary, as soon as bobbins near the bottom of the pillow. Bobbins should never be allowed to hang off the pillow or the tension will be spoiled.

PATTERN 6
FAN AND
ROSEGROUND MAT

In Torchon lace, square and round mats are usually worked in four sections as indicated in the working diagram.

11 prs bobbins with ½yd (0.5m) per bobbin.
2 weavers with 1yd (1m) on each.

1. Hang four prs in order right to left at a.
2. Hang one pr on each of the support pins b, c, d and e.
3. Use the first two prs on the left to cover the pin with WS and twist.
4. Using the RH pr and WS work to R through two prs on a and through pr on support pin b. Twist weavers and place pin 1.
5. Working to L, WS through three prs,

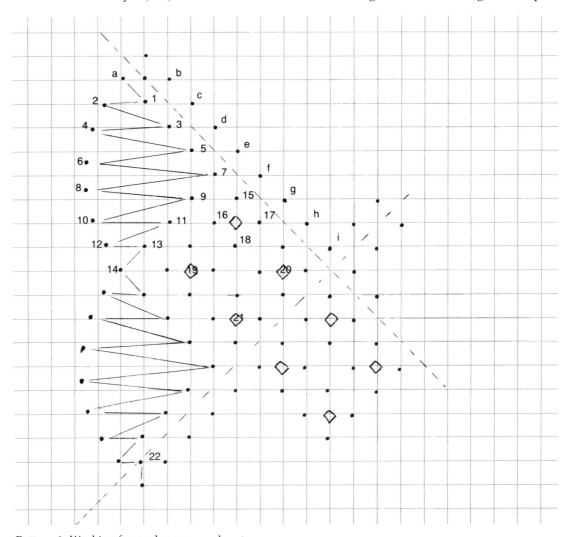

Pattern 6. Working fan and roseground mat.

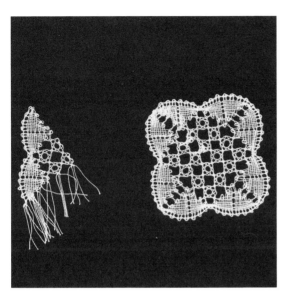

A section of a fan and roseground mat and
a finished mat.

twist weavers once and WS and twist with
edge pr. Place pin 2.

6. Cover pin with WS and twist and work
to R through prs in fan and pr on pin c.

7. Continue fan until pin 7 is placed.

8. Twist all passive prs in fan.

9. Take weavers back to 8 and work pin.

10. Remove support pins b, c, d and e
and pull loops into fan.

11. Complete fan to pin 14 as described
in Fan Edging (see Pattern 5, page 55).
Check there are four prs at 14 and one pr
against each fan pin 7, 9, 11 and 13.

Roseground
- There are many different rosegrounds but
all follow the same basic working plan.
- Four holes are used and these are indicated
by a diamond marking on the pricking.
- Four prs are used to work the holes, two
prs moving diagonally from each side.
- Before working the holes, the prs must be
prepared.

To Work Roseground

1. Sort out the prs from pins 7 and 9 and
push the remaining prs to the left.

2. Take two new prs and hang them on f
and g.

3. To prepare the pairs, work WS and
twist with the prs from 7 and 9. Place no
pins.

4. Work WS and twist with the pairs
from f and g. Place no pins. This is one of
the few occasions when prs side by side
are worked together.

5. There are now four prs ready to work
15, 16, 17 and 18 in sequence.

6. *Numbering from L, work HS with
prs 2 and 3. Place pin 15 and HS to cover
pin.

7. Work prs 1 and 2 in HS, pin, HS at 16.

8. Work prs 3 and 4 in HS, pin, HS at 17.

9. Work prs 2 and 3 in HS, pin, HS at
18.**

10. Complete the roseground by working WS and twist with pr from 16 and LH
prs from 18. Place no pin.

11. WS and twist RH pr from 18 and pr
from 17. Remove support pins from f and
g and pull loops into roseground. The
roseground is complete.

12. Prepare prs from 11 and 13 with WS
and twist. Prs from 16 and 18 are already
prepared and roseground 19 can be completed by working the sequence * to **.

13. To work roseground 20, use prs
from support pins h and i, prepared with
WS and twist, and prs from 17 and 18
already prepared. Remove support pins.

14. Complete roseground 21 in a similar
manner.

15. Work next fan using four prs at 14
and taking in prs from roseground 19 and
21 in sequence.

16. Work pin 22, to turn corner, as
described in pattern 5, (see page 56).

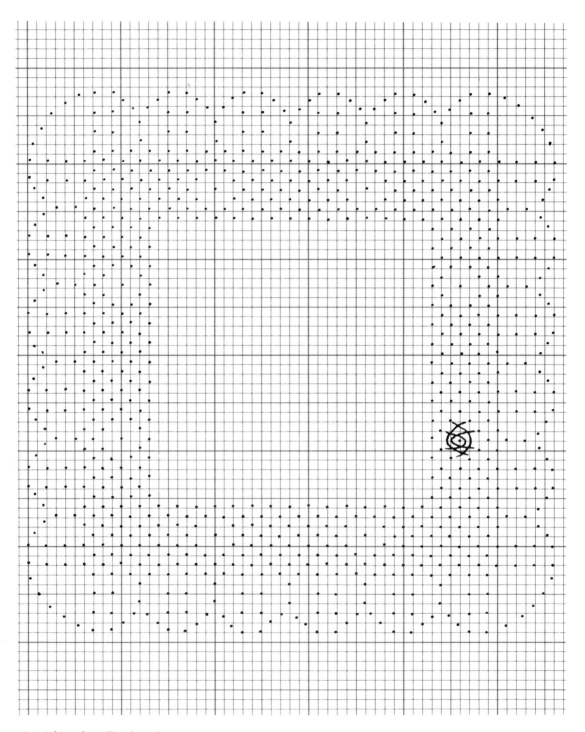

A pricking for a Torchon fan and spider.

17. Turn pillow, reposition cover cloth and bobbins and work next section of square.

18. Gradually push all pins down into pricking so that the cover cloth can be used properly and the threads move freely.

19. Cover the worked pins with a piece of cellulose acetate as well as the cloth. This allows a view of the work without the threads catching on the pins.

20. When all the sections are worked, sewings must be made with the appropriate prs into positions a, 1, 3, 5, 7 etc. and the work completed as previously described.

Roseground Variations

Preparation	At Pin-Holes
1. Whole stitch and twist	Half stitch, pin, half stitch (described in detail above)
2. Half stitch	Half stitch, pin, half stitch
3. Whole stitch and twist	Whole stitch and twist, pin whole stitch and twist
4. Half stitch	Whole stitch and twist, pin, whole stitch and twist

PATTERN 7
TORCHON FAN AND SPIDER EDGING

12 prs bobbins with 1yd (1m) per bobbin. Weaver pair with 5yds (5m) per bobbin. The weavers could be a contrasting colour.

1. Hang one pr each on support pins a to h and two prs astride on i.

2. Use prs from a and b to work pin 1 in HS, pin, HS.

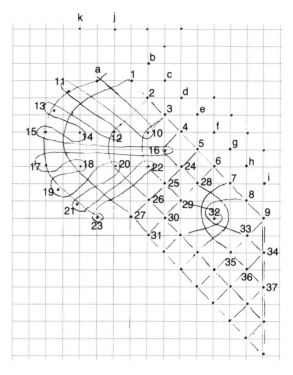

Pattern 7. Working Torchon fans and spiders.

3. Remove pins a and b. Work down line from 2 to 8 working HS ground. Work footside at 9 with two prs on i. Remove support pins.

The Torchon Fan (worked in WS and twist)

4. Hang weavers at j and final pair at k.

5. Work WS and twist with prs from j and k. Place pin a and cover.

6. The weavers should be the RH pair. Continue to R through prs from 1, 2 and 3 and place pin 10.

7. Work L through four prs. Place pin 11.

8. Cover pin and work two prs to pin 12. (One pr has been left at 10.)

9. Continue number sequence to 15

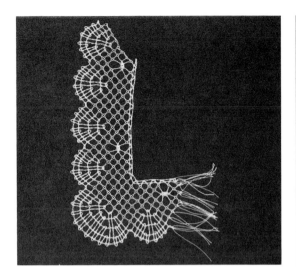

A torchon fan and spider edging.

A torchon fan and spider complete mat.

leaving prs at 12 and 14 and ending with the weavers and edge pair to work 15.

10.   WS and twist from 15 through prs left at 14, 12 and 10. Work through pair from 4 and place pin 16.

11.   Take weavers back to 17.

12.   Work 18 to 23 in sequence.

13.   Work 24 to 27 HS, pin, HS using pr from 5 and prs from fan. Check – you should have two prs left at 23.

14.   Continue with ground stitches from 28 to 31.

15.   Make a spider at 32 using prs from 7, 8, 28 and 29.

16.   Work ground stitches at 33, 35, and 36 and footsides at 34 and 37.

17.   Continue filling in ground and foot-sides until one pattern repeat is completed and the prs are available for the next fan.

18.   Pins 27 and 31 are equivalent to 1 and 2 at the beginning of the work.

19.   Complete square and make sewings as previously described.

20.   Mount on suitable fabric.

PATTERN 8
ELONGATED DIAMONDS AND SPIDER BOOKMARK

16 prs bobbins with ¾yd (0.75m) per bobbin.

1.   Hang two prs astride a. Twist RH prs twice and cover with WS and twist.

2.   Hang one pr each on support pins b to g.

3.   Work HS, pin, HS down diagonal from 1 to 6. Remove support pins.

4.   Work 7 to 12 using pr from h to m. Remove support pins.

To Make The False Footside

1.   Hang two prs astride 13. Work as a.

2.   Take RH pr from 13 and WS and twist through prs at 1 to 6. No pins are used. Tension as best you can.

3.   Take LH prs from 13 and work in similar manner through prs from 7 to 12.

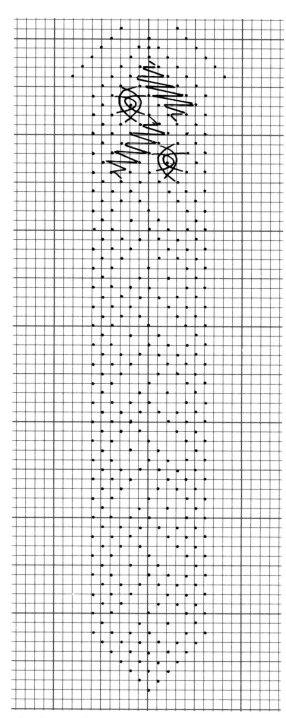

An elongated diamond and spider
bookmark pricking.

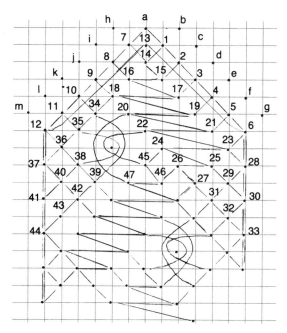

Pattern 8. Working diamonds and spiders.

The Elongated Diamond

1. You have already practised
diamonds. The elongated diamond is
begun in a similar manner.
2. Work pin 14 in WS with prs from 1
and 7. The diamond continues in the
normal manner to pin 18. At this point,
prs are left out at 18, 20, 22, 24 and 26 but
continue to be taken in at 19, 21 and 23.
3. At 23 and 25 prs will be left out.

> **Check**
> There should be two prs remaining to work 27.

4. At 28 work a footside using prs from
23, 6 and the false footside pr from 13.
5. Work 29, 31 and 32 as ground and 30
and 33 as footsides.

67

6. Return to L of strip and work 34, 35 and 36 as ground. 37 will be a footside using prs from 35, 12 and the false footside pr from 13.

The Spider

Spiders are made as in the spider bookmark. In this pattern, only four prs are involved. On two edges the legs come from and go back into the ground. On the other two edges they come from a diamond and return into a diamond.

7. Make spider using prs from 20, 22, 34 and 35.
8. Secure LH legs at 38 and 39.
9. Complete ground as appropriate to 44.

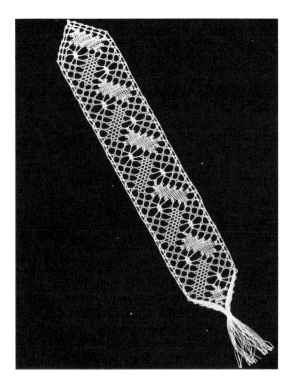

A diamond and spider bookmark.

Note The next diamond is elongated in the opposite direction and worked in HS. Pairs taken in at 45 and 47 are spider's legs.

10. Complete this half stitch diamond and the ground and footside beyond before returning to the RH side for more ground, footside and a spider.
11. Complete as instructed in diamond strip.

PATTERN 9
HALF STITCH TRAIL
AND ROSEGROUND STRIP

15 prs bobbins with ¾yd (0.75m) per bobbin.

1. Set up point and false footside as for the elongated diamond and spider strip.
Note The trail starts in the same manner as the elongated diamond but then travels diagonally from one side to the other in the work.
2. Work in number sequence as far as 25 but do not place pin 25.
Note At angle pin 23, no prs enter or leave the trail.
3. Work pins 26, 27 and 28 as ground and footside.
4. Work a footside at 29. This will stop you taking the pr left out at 24 back into the trail when it continues.
5. Before the trail is continued rosegrounds must be worked at 30 and 31. Remind yourself of the sequence for roseground by turning to the fan and roseground mat (*see* pages 62–65).
6. For 30 prepare prs from 19 and 21. Prepare prs from 26 and 27.
7. Work roseground 30. Do not forget to complete the roseground by working

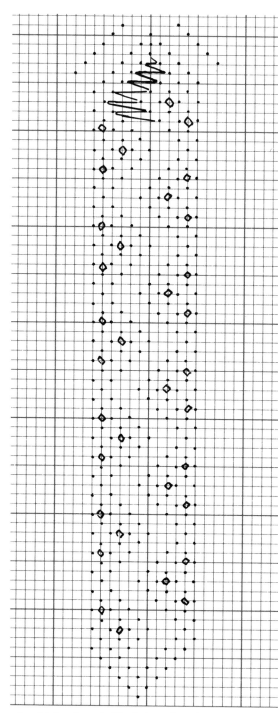

A pricking for a half stitch trail and roseground strip.

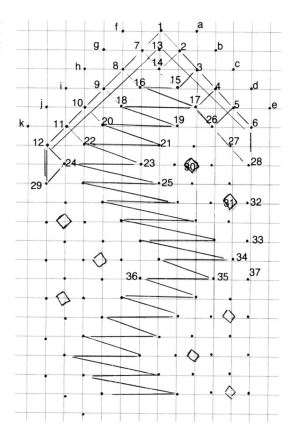

Pattern 9. Working trail and roseground.

each set of prs together after placing the bottom pin.

8.   Roseground 31 uses two prs from 30 and the inner two prs from footside 28 which are already prepared.

9.   As this roseground is at a footside, work the first two holes normally and at 32 work a footside. Work the bottom hole normally.

10.   After completing the RH side of 31 the remaining pr on the R can be worked and a footside completed at 33.

11.   Return to the trail. The weavers are at the RH edge of the trail. Take them through the LH pr from roseground 30 and place pin 25.

12. Continue the trail taking prs in from the roseground on the right and leaving them out on the left to work the next patch of rosegrounds.

13. Work as far as 36; do not place pin.

14. Use pr from 34 to make footside 37.

15. Work three rosegrounds on LH side of strip.

Check you have prepared pairs. The outer pins are worked as footsides.

16. Continue the trail. The weavers are the LH pair in the trail. Work them through one roseground pr and place 36.

17. Work to R but remember to leave a pr at 35.

18. Continue alternate patches of roseground and trail.

19. Finish at point as previously instructed.

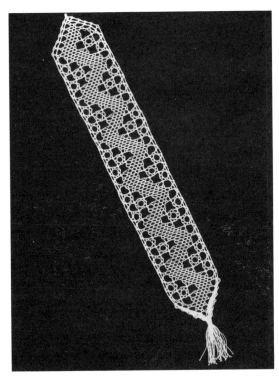

A trail and roseground strip.

PATTERN 10   GIMP AND ROSEGROUND BOOKMARK

The gimp thread will emphasize the areas of roseground and diamonds.

18 prs bobbins with ¾yd (0.75m) per bobbin.
1 gimp pair with ¾yd (0.75m) between the pair.
Cotton Perle 5 or 8 are suitable. I used Cotton Perle 5.

1. Hang prs on support pins and work HS pin HS from 1 to 15.

2. Hang two prs at side of work and work WS and twist through all prs from L to R to form false footside.

3. At RH side make footside at 16. The pair at 15 and the false footside pair are already worked. Place a pin inside two prs and cover it with the second and third pr from the right.

4. Use pr from 13 and 14 with HS pin HS at 17 and so on back across to the L.

5. At 18 use prs from 1 and 2 and false footside pr for footside at 18, again by placing the pin inside two prs. Remove support pins.

6. Fill in all footside and ground stitches up to the gimp line.

The Gimp

1. The gimp is usually held between the threads of a pr with two twists before and after the gimp.

2. The prs involved at 1 to 12 already have one twist and must all be twisted again.

3. Hang the gimp pr on a support pin at 13.

4. Pass the gimp from L to R through prs

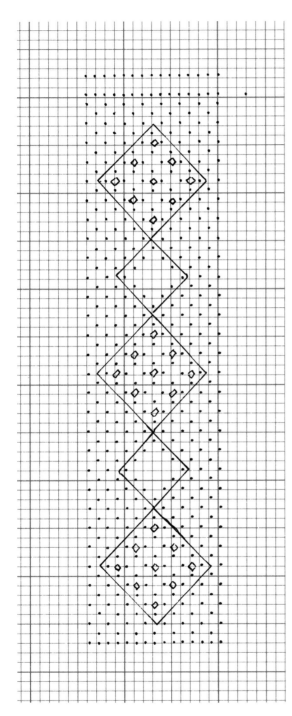

A pricking for a gimp and roseground bookmark.

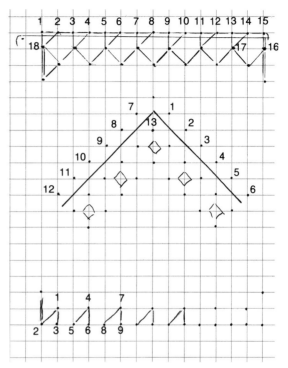

Pattern 10. Setting up a straight edge and working the gimp and roseground motif. Finishing at a straight edge.

1 to 6 by weaving it under the first thread and over the second of each pr.

5. Twist prs 1 to 6 twice to hold the gimp in position.

6. Now pass the gimp from R to L through prs 7 to 12 by weaving it over the first thread and under the second of each pr.

7. Twist prs 7 to 12 to hold the gimp in position.

8. Remove support pin 13.

9. The roseground can now be worked as described in pattern 6, (see page 62).

10. Prepare prs 1 and 2, 3 and 4, 5 and 6, 7 and 8, 9 and 10, 11 and 12. Work each area of roseground in turn making sure of good tension. The gimp should run in a straight line.

A gimp and roseground bookmark.

11. When the roseground is complete, pass the gimp threads towards each other in the manner described.

12. At the bottom of the diamond shape the two gimp threads must cross each other. Some books say 'Pass right over left', others say 'Pass left over right'. I do not think it matters as long as you are consistent.

Quick Reference for Gimps
- Passing left to right: under first thread and over second.
- Passing right to left: over first thread and under second.

13. When the diamond of roseground and gimp is complete, two areas of

ground and footside must be worked, up to the next gimp line.

14. Pass the gimps through the appropriate prs and pull them well to give a good outline to the roseground. Work the whole stitch diamond.

15. Pass the gimps below the diamond and cross them.

16. Complete the next area of ground and footside followed by further roseground. Watch the tension of the gimp.

17. After the last area of roseground has been completed the gimp must be fastened off. Cross the gimps as before and take the LH thread up the RH side of the diamond and the RH thread up the LH side of the diamond so that there is a double gimp through at least four prs held in position by twists.

18. When the next row of ground has been worked the tension of the gimp should be checked.

19. Complete work down to final line of holes.

20. Take LH pr from 1 as weavers and work WS through two prs from footside, twist twice and put up pin 2. WS to R through two prs and leave.

21. Take RH pr from 1 as new weavers and work WS to L through three prs. Put up pin 3 and work back through two prs and leave.

22. Take LH pr from 4 and work to L through four prs. Place pin 5 and work back through two prs.

23. There are now five prs accumulated at the end of the lace. Pick up the fourth pr from the L and lift them back across the lace in a north-westerly direction.

24. Take the RH pr from 4 and work L through four prs. Place pin 6 and work back through two prs.

25. Throw fourth pr from L out of work as previously explained.

26. Keeping a good tension work along the edge of the lace towards the right in similar manner.

27. For the last hole there will be two prs from the RH footside. Take the LH pr through two prs to the left and leave. Take the RH pr through all prs, place last pin and WS to other edge. Check tension of all prs and tie weavers securely to make a tight bundle. Correct the tension.

28. The remaining bobbins may now be cut off leaving a short tassel.

29. Alternatively they may be laid towards the left above the narrow braid you have first created and between the threads of the last and last-but-one thrown out pairs. These pairs can be knotted around all the remaining prs so that they are tied to the braid. Pressing down the pins on the corner will help you to see what you are doing.

30. Cut off the bobbins including those which were thrown out as the braid was constructed and the two gimp bobbins.

31. Remove pins from the lace and trim ends, including gimps, close to work without cutting knots.

PATTERN 11
LAVENDER BAG

24 prs bobbins with 2½yds (2.5m) per bobbin and 5yds (5m) on each of the weavers.

The four prs which hang at the top of the fan can be of a contrasting colour.

1. As with the fan and roseground mat this mat is worked in four sections.
2. Hang four prs in order at the top of the fan and one pr on each support pin above the edge of the fan.
3. Decide which type of fan you wish to

make from the selection in the fan edging photograph.

4. Follow instructions for the fan and roseground mat for making the fan. Remove support pins.

5. Hang more prs on support pins and form the edge of the spider with HS, pin HS. Remove support pins.

6. Make three-legged spider with pairs added and pairs from fan.

7. Complete edge of spider and make next fan.

8. Hang four prs on support pins and make a patch of four rosegrounds. Remember to take out support pins.

9. Either work diagonally to R and work next group of four rosegrounds or work to L and make next spider and fan.

10. Continue until the segment is complete to the end of the fifth fan.

11. Work pin to change position of weavers for next fan.

12. Turn pillow and rearrange cover cloth. Remember to twist on the pairs across the corner before they enter the next fan.

13. As work progresses push pins in.

14. If you have insufficient pins for the whole piece leave in as many as possible, especially those holding the fan in position. All the threads will gather the lace and spoil its shape if given the chance.

15. When work is complete, make sewings. Finish off as previously described.

16. You have now completed a piece of lace which makes an attractive mat. To make a lavender bag a further square mat will be needed.

17. The choice of stitch in this mat could be roseground, half stitch ground or in the case of my sample, whole stitch and twist. The outer edge is kept firm with a footside.

18. The lace is again made in segments.

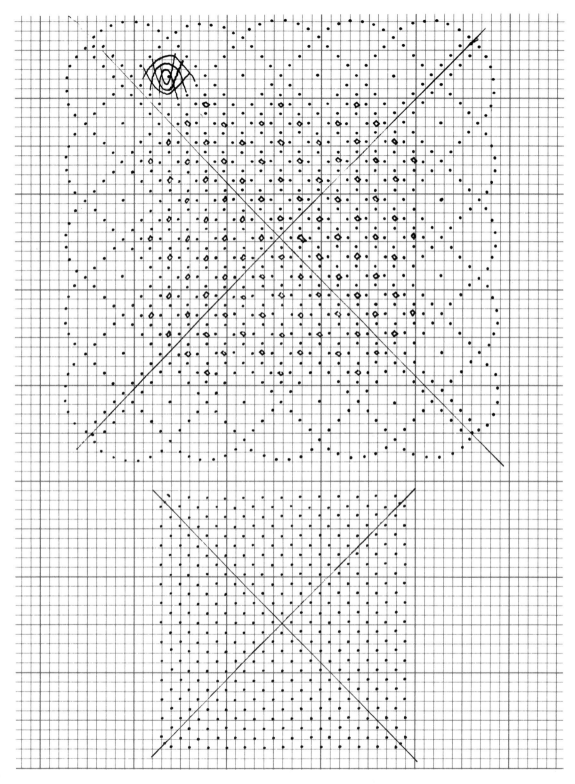

Lavender bag prickings.

Setting up a Footside and Ground on the Left

15 prs bobbins with ½yd (0.5m) per bobbin.

1.   Hang two prs at a. Twist RH pr twice. Cover pin with WS and twist.
2.   Leave LH pr and work WS and twist with RH pr and pr on b. Do not place a pin.
3.   Use RH pr and pr from c to make WS and twist before and after pin 1.
4.   Continue down diagonal making stitches at 2, 3, 4 etc. Remove support pins.
5.   Making footsides where necessary fill in quarter segment of square.

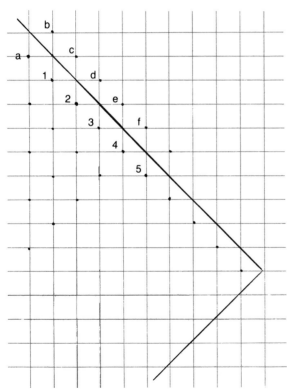

Pattern 11. Working a square with the footside on the left.

Lace for a lavender bag.

6.   Turn corner and work next section, pushing in pins as necessary.
7.   Complete square and make sewings. Finish in the desired way.
8.   Make a small bag approximately 2¼in (5.7cm) square from fabric or ribbon to hold the lavender or pot-pourri. Stitch the opening to seal the lavender inside.
9.   Place the bag on the wrong side of the large mat in a central position.
10.   Place the square mat wrong-side down on the lavender bag and fasten both pieces of lace together by weaving narrow ribbon or embroidery cotton through the mesh of the lace.
11.   The ends can be tied in a neat bow at

The completed lavender bag.

one corner of the bag on the right side of the larger section.

12.   Colours which tone or contrast can be selected for the fan edge, lavender bag and ribbon.

PATTERN 12
TRIANGLES, SPIDERS
AND HONEYCOMB
SAMPLER

Triangles are one of the least-used motifs in Torchon, with the result that horizontal and vertical lines within the design do not occur very often.

   This pattern also contains two types of spiders and a patch of honeycomb. It also describes a method of getting rid of ends. The pattern requires 18 pairs.

1.   Hang two prs at a and one pr on each of support pins b to o; hang a further footside pair on h and o.

2.   Make a whole stitch diamond as previously described, removing support pins as you go and taking in the two prs from h and o.

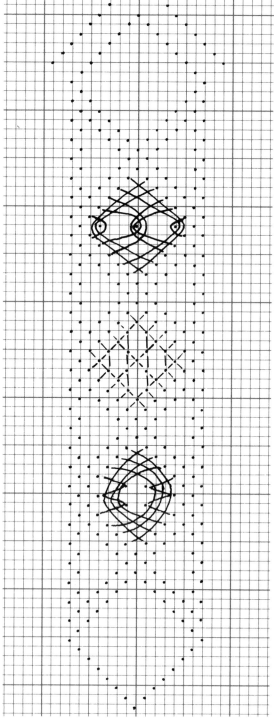

A pricking for triangles, spider and honeycomb sampler.

76

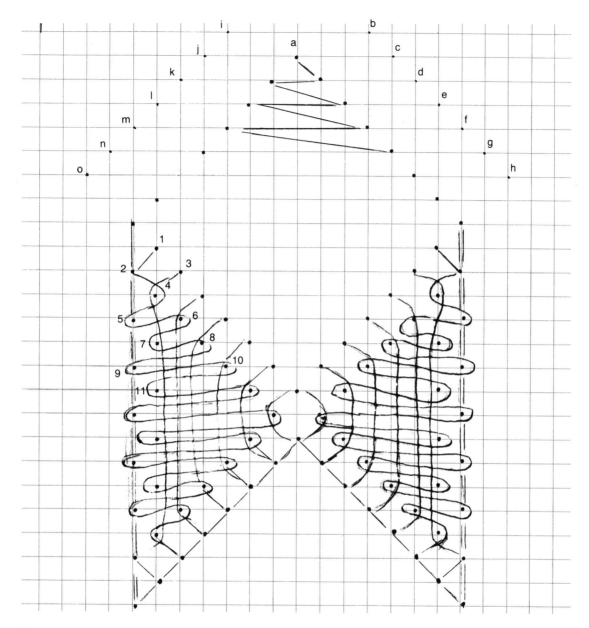

Pattern 12. Working triangles.

3. When all the pairs are in the diamond at its widest part, twist all the passives once.
4. Complete the diamond leaving out two prs on each of the pins at its widest part (these will be needed for the footside) and one pair on each of the other pins.

To Make the LH Triangle

1. Take the pair from the diamond at 1 and work a footside at 2.
2. Take the inner pr and WS with diamond pr 3. Twist RH pr twice. It will be the weaver for the triangle. Place pin 4.

3. Use weaver to make footside at 5.

4. Take inner pr and work to R through one pr and take in pr from diamond. Place pin 6.

5. Work to L through two prs. Twist weavers twice and place pin 7.

6. Work to R through two prs and new pr from diamond. Twist and place 8.

7. Work to L through three prs and make footside at 9.

8. Take inner pr and work to R through three prs and new pr from diamond. Place pin 10.

9. Work to L through four pairs and twist weavers. Place pin 11.

10. Have another look at the photograph on page 80. The pins placed at 7 and 11 are called snatch pins. They are used when no new prs are added or left out. In a triangle they alternate with the footside pins down the vertical edge and make a parallel line with the footside.

11. Continue taking in prs from the diamond and working snatch pins and footsides alternately.

12. When the widest part of the triangle is reached pairs are left out at each pin as the triangle becomes narrower. The vertical edge continues as before.

13. The RH triangle is worked as a mirror image of the LH one (see page 80).

14. When both triangles are complete, a variation on a spider can be worked.

15. Use ground stitches to complete the upper edge of the diamond shape.

Spider A

1. Complete 1 to 13 in ground stitches (HS pin HS).

2. Twist prs from 6 and 12 once and all other prs three times.

3. Pass 8 through 2, 3, 4 and 5.

4. Pass 9 through 2, 3, 4 and 5.

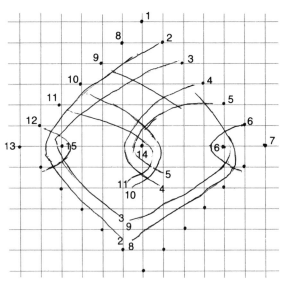

Working spider A.

5. Pass 10 through 2 and 3.

6. Pass 11 through 2 and 3.

7. Twist 4, 5, 10 and 11 three times and use them to work a basic spider at 14. (See pattern 4, page 53).

8. Work 12 through 2 and 3 to 15 and back through 3 and 2.

9. Work 6 through 8 and 9 to 16 and back through 9 and 8.

10. Work 5 through 9 and 8.

11. Work 4 through 9 and 8.

12. Work 3 through 11, 10, 9 and 8.

13. Work 2 through 11, 10, 9 and 8.

14. Twist all prs as before, securing them in the diamond.

15. Work the next triangles on each side.

16. The next diamond space contains an area of honeycomb.

The Honeycomb Diamond

1. Work pins 1 to 13 in HS. Pin HS with appropriate prs. The area is now ready for honeycomb which is worked in two lines. The first line goes down the diagonal as before, taking appropriate prs in turn. The

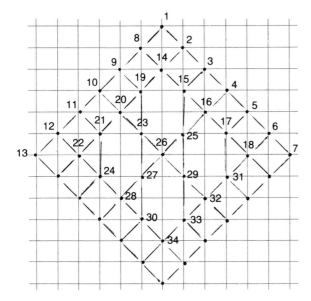

Working honeycomb.

second broken line is worked with prs which lie next to each other, one pair coming in at 45 degrees and the pair hanging vertically down the work. The stitch used is HS and twist pin HS and twist.

2. Following the diagram work 14 to 22 in honeycomb stitch using appropriate prs.

3. Look at the diagram and think of 14, 19, 20, 21 and 22 as the first line of the pattern.

4. For the second broken line, use prs from 19 and 20 to work 23 and prs from 21 and 22 to work 24.

5. Now make a continuous line. Prs from 15 and 16 for 25.

6. LH pr from 25 and RH pr from 23 for 26.

7. LH pr from 26 and LH pr from 23 for 27.

8. LH pr from 27 and RH pr from 24 for 28.

9. The next line is broken. Prs from 25 and 26 make 29. Prs from 27 and 28 make 30.

10. The next line is continuous with appropriate prs working 31, 32 and 33.

11. The bottom hole 34 is worked with prs from 30 and 33.

12. The honeycomb area is now complete.

13. Complete the diamond shape with ground stitches followed by the next triangle on each side. This is followed by another spider variation.

Spider B

1. This spider has five legs on each side. Twist the prs from 1, 2, 3, 4, 5, 6, 7 and 8 three times. Twist prs from 9 and 10 once.

2. WS 5 through 1, 2, 3 and 4.

3. WS 6 through 1, 2, 3 and 4.

4. WS 7 through 1, 2, 3 and 4.

5. WS 8 through 1, 2 and 3 and place pin 11.

6. WS back through 3, 2 and 1.

7. 8 now works a HS pin HS at 12 with 10.

8. LH pr from 12 will be secured in the base of the diamond at 14 when the spider is complete.

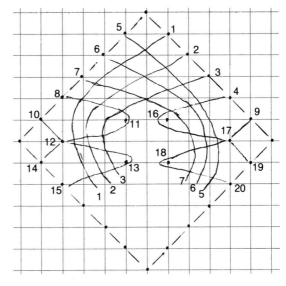

Working spider B.

The completed sampler.

9. RH pr from 12 works back through 1, 2 and 3 and pin 13 is placed. Work back through 3, 2 and 1. Thus pr which started at 8 will finally be secured in the diamond at 15.

10. Complete RH side to same level in like manner. 4 through 5, 6 and 7 to 16, back to 17 worked in HS pin HS with 9. Back to 18 and secured at 19 and 20.

11. To complete the spider take 3 through 7, 6 and 5. Take 2 through 7, 6 and 5. Take 1 through 7, 6 and 5.

12. Twist prs from 12 and 17 once. Twist all other prs three times.

13. Complete the diamond shape with ground stitches.

14. Work the next triangle on each side as previously described.

15. Work the final diamond shape in whole stitch, twisting the passives at the widest part and throwing out pairs as the diamond narrows.

16. Reef knot and cut off all the prs. Remove pins.

17. Both diamonds can be folded in half towards the wrong side on the twist line, thus forming triangles at the top and the bottom of the sampler.

18. The edges can be neatly stitched together and cut threads can be tucked inside the triangle to give a neat finish.

5 Mounting Lace

If you have taken several weeks or even months to make a piece of lace, it is worth taking time and trouble over mounting it. It is a process which fills some lacemakers with dread. However, if you plunge in and have a go your skill should increase with experience. Try to make a rule that as you finish each piece you mount it.

POINTS TO CONSIDER

1.   The fabric should be of good quality because the lace will almost certainly out-live the mounting.
2.   The lace, fabric and sewing thread should preferably be of the same fibre. However, it is sometimes difficult to get suitable fabric and it seems that putting cotton on linen or vice versa is now acceptable.
3.   The lace, fabric and thread should be of similar weight so that one enhances the other. This again is a debatable point. I recently entered a tray-cloth in a competition thinking that the fabric was a little too fine. The judge commented that it was not fine enough.
4.   Straight edges of lace must be lined up on the grain of the fabric even though the finish may not be hem-stitched. The eye is drawn to any unevenness, especially at corners.
5.   In shaped lace the grain in both directions should be marked with a tacking thread so that the lace design rests on the fabric in a pleasing way.

6.   Ready-made handkerchief squares are available from suppliers but these rarely seem the correct size for the edging you wish to mount. Remember that you can ease lace on to a square which is slightly small but you cannot stretch it on to a square that is too large.
7.   The fabric and lace may shrink at different rates when laundered.
8.   All of the lace or none of the lace should be on the mounting fabric.

PREPARATION FOR MOUNTING

1.   If the grain of the fabric does not appear 'square' pull it into shape.
2.   Shrink the fabric and the lace by pressing with a damp cloth. Beware of scorches. Make sure everything is clean. Stains on the ironing board cover can be transferred to the damp lace.
3.   Decide how wide the hems are to be. Handkerchief hems may be ¼in (6mm) wide, while ½in (13mm) or more would be suitable for tray-cloths and table-cloths. Convention makes a handkerchief with a ½in (13mm) hem look like a table mat no matter how fine the lace.

ATTACHING STRAIGHT-EDGE LACE

There are many traditional ways of attaching lace to fabric. Details can be

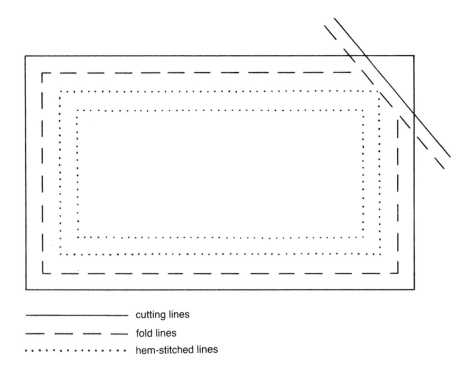

cutting lines

— — — — fold lines

• • • • • • • • • • hem-stitched lines

A diagram showing the lines mentioned in the text.

found in sewing and embroidery books and other lace books. Fine work can be attached to a rolled hem. Hem-stitched hems have a good crisp appearance. Corners can be mitred or overlapped. For overlapped corners the long sides should be turned on to the short sides.

The following method gives a neat hem-stitched finish and the mat is created as the lace is attached. You need enough fabric without a selvedge to fill the space in the lace and turnings plus extra for trimming especially if the fabric will fray. The turning of the hem is the same width as the hem so that no shadow or ridge is created.

Order of Work

1. Sit the edging squarely on the shrunken fabric, wrong side of lace to right side of fabric. Carefully draw a thread from the fabric level with the footside on one edge of the lace. Use a needle and ease the thread out of the full width.

2. Making sure that one edge of the lace is on this line, draw out a second thread at right angles and level with a second side of the lace.

3. Line two edges of the lace with these drawn lines and draw out a third thread level with a third side.

4. Draw a fourth thread to complete the shape.

5. If you have been accurate, all four footside edges should be sitting on drawn lines.

6. Tack the lace evenly to the fabric and hem-stitch the footsides to the drawn line.

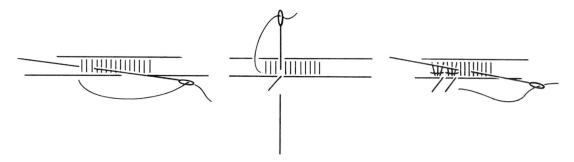

Making a hem-stitched edge.

7. Measure the width of the proposed hem from the hem-stitched line towards the centre of the fabric and withdraw another four threads, drawing them out until the lines meet at the corners.

8. Remove tackings, turn the lace over and use an iron to press the turnings away from the lace and over the fabric.

9. These turnings must be trimmed back so that they are twice the width of the hem. Measure, draw out a thread and trim on the drawn line.

10. Fold the turning in half and press the hem in position.

11. Trim and mitre the corners if desired, otherwise fold the long sides over the short sides.

12. Tack the hem in position and hem-stitch it along the drawn line.

13. Remove tacking and press.

Mounting by hem-stitching.

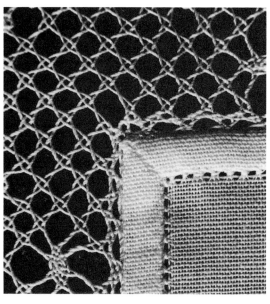

A mitred corner.

Alternative Straight-Edge Mounting

1. Use a suitably sized ready-made mount or make one to the required size either with a rolled or hem-stitched hem.
2. As the mat is approximately the same size as the lace, tacking is not possible. Try pinning the lace to the fabric at the corners and at one or two points along each edge to give even distribution. Make stitches into the fold of the hem and the footside alternately so that the lace is well secured and neat. This is best done from the wrong side. Some books advocate oversewing.

Making a Rolled Hem

1. Rolled hems are most successful with very fine lawn.
2. Pull the fabric into shape and shrink it with a damp cloth.
3. I find it best to create the mounting and attach the lace at the same time, using two separate threads and needles. In this

A rolled hem.

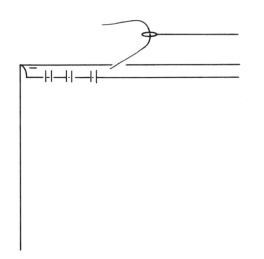

Working a rolled hem.

way a more accurate fit can be achieved.
4. Draw out the threads at right angles to each other on two of the edges and trim the fabric to those lines.
5. Press a single turning ⅛in (3mm) deep on each of those edges.
6. Take a threaded needle and knot at the end. If you are right-handed you will work from right to left. If you are left-handed you will work from left to right.
7. About 1½in (38mm) from the corner, slide the needle under the turning and bring it out through the fold of the hem so the knot is under the turning and the thread secure.
8. Make a stitch ¼in (6mm) long along the line of the fold.
9. Make a very small stitch in the main fabric directly below the thread's exit point.
10. Make another ¼in (6mm) stitch in the fold, starting very close to the exit point of the first stitch.

11.   Take another small stitch in the main fabric.

12.   Repeat this sequence until about an inch has been worked and with the thread at the folded edge.

13.   Holding the mounting firmly, gently pull the sewing thread in the direction in which you are working and the fabric should roll over on itself to form a neat hem. Continue as before.

14.   When you are ¼in (6mm) from the corner, manipulate the needle under the turning of the next side and out of what will be the corner of the handkerchief. Continue to make the rolled hem along the second side, using the needle to tuck in and make a neat corner.

15.   When several inches of hem are completed around one corner, you can begin to attach the lace. Line the corner of the lace with the corner of the mounting and use pins to hold the lace in position.

16.   Using another knotted thread and needle, slide the needle up to the outer edge of the hem so that the knot is within the hem.

17.   Make small stitches through the footside of the lace and into the outer edge of the hem alternately so that the lace is neatly secured.

18.   Make hem and attach lace alternately, up and around the first corner.

19.   As you approach the second corner estimate where the fabric must be cut and draw a thread. Trim back to that line.

Keep the lace well away from the scissors. Remember you can ease lace to a mounting which is too small but cannot stretch it to a mounting that is too large.

20.   Turn the hem and attach the lace down the third side and when you approach the next corner, draw a thread and trim as before.

21.   The extent of the mounting is now decided and the hem can be complete.

22.   The remaining lace which is not always completely 'square' can now be attached to the remaining edges.

23.   When the attaching is completed, finish off both threads securely.

24.   Press the mounting and lace to give a neat, flat finish.

MOUNTING A SHAPED EDGE

If the finished lace has a scalloped or round inner edge it will not be possible to make a hem on which the lace can be attached. There are a variety of methods which may be employed.

Using Pin-Stitch or Punch-Stitch

1.   You will need sufficient fabric for it to extend 1in (25mm) under the lace all the way round.

2.   Use a coloured tacking thread to mark

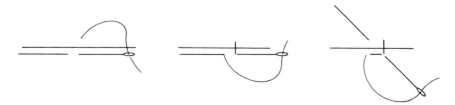

Pin-stitch.

Pin-stitch.

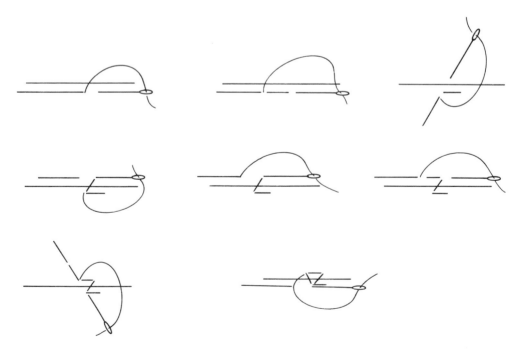

Three-sided punch-stitch.

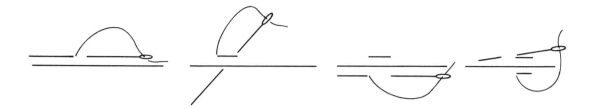

Four-sided punch-stitch.

the grain of the fabric in both directions at the centre of the fabric.

3. Shrink the lace and fabric as previously described.

4. On a flat surface, place the lace on the fabric, wrong side of lace to right side of fabric, so that the grain of the fabric looks right in relation to the design.

5. On a scalloped inner edge, the inner and outer edges of the scallops should be on straight threads.

6. Tack the lace to the fabric fairly near the footside, making sure that the fabric remains flat.

7. The lace can now be attached to the fabric using either pin-stitch or one of the punch-stitches.

8. A fairly thick needle can be used and by gently pulling the sewing thread a pattern of holes can be produced.

9. Practise the stitches before embarking on the lace.

10. Only the footside should be stitched and the moving forward bulk of the stitches should be in the fabric.

11. When the attachment has been completed, turn the mat over and carefully cut away the excess fabric fairly close to the stitching line.

12. If the fabric is fine enough and your fingers nimble enough, a wider margin may be left and this used to make a narrow hem.

13. Press the completed mat.

Using a Buttonholed Edge

1. Place the shrunk lace on the shrunk fabric in a pleasing manner.

2. Draw on the fabric round the edge of the lace to be attached with a water-soluble pen.

3. Remove the lace and you should have a pattern of its shape on the fabric.

4. Use blanket-stitch or buttonhole stitch close together to edge this shape. The knots of the stitches should fall on the marked line.

5. Remove the marked line with a damp cloth.

6. Carefully cut away the excess fabric as close as possible to the stitched edge.

7. Place the lace back in position and attach the footside to the knots on the edge of the blanket stitch. Distribute the lace evenly using pins as markers.

8. Press the completed mat.

The methods described so far attach lace to an edge and all the lace is exposed and over the edge of the fabric. There are occasions when a piece of lace is attached to fabric and the colour of the fabric rather than the light will expose its design. This could happen if the lace is to be framed in some way or if for example it is to run across a pillowcase or towel.

In these cases the lace must be tacked into position on the fabric and then hemmed or running-stitched into position so that the stitches do not show and spoil the design. If the lace is to be placed into a permanent frame or paperweight, these stitches need to be few and far between and may not be necessary if threads from sewings are used. See note on sewings. If the lace is to decorate the end of a pillow-case, the side seams of the pillowcase can be opened up and both ends of the lace can be sewn within the seams. This will dispose of the fringe of ends where the bobbins have been cut off. Selvedges can be constructed on both ends of a strip of lace. These can be made into narrow hems and all ends can be hidden within one of these hems.

PRESSING LACE

After mounting, lace needs to be well pressed to give a good finish. It is best to press it when damp, using either water or spray starch which gives a crisp finish.

The damp article should be gently pulled into shape, with the wrong side upwards.

Articles with corners should be pressed firmly across well-squared corners. Next, the sides should be pressed and finally the centre of the fabric. For articles in which the mounting is shaped, pressing should begin with the straight grain in the centre of the mount, gradually working towards the edge. You may find when you have mounted using pin-stitch and punch-stitch that the fabric has stretched and appears much larger than the space it is to occupy. However with damping and gentle pulling on the stitched area you will find that it can be shrunk to fit flat.

If the pressing is done on the wrong side, a lovely matt surface will develop on the right side. This is particularly so with linen and enhances the lace. Pin-stitched and punch-stitched edges benefit from being pressed from the wrong side into a soft surface. This gives a raised appearance to the stitching which again shows the lace to advantage.

6   Pattern Adaptation

The processes learned in Chapter 4 can now be used to work more complicated pieces of lace, referring back, as necessary, to the appropriate pattern. Besides making our own interpretations we can also change the size of the lace, either by using a different-sized graph paper or by photocopying to a different size.

The two main sizes of graph paper available are 10 squares to 25mm and 2mm or 20 squares to 20mm.

The lavender bag in this chapter is drafted on 2mm paper. Compare it with the lavender bag in Pattern 11 in Chapter 4 which is drafted on 10 squares to 25mm paper. Both prickings are identical in the number of dots they contain.

The lace in this chapter is worked in a variety of threads. This lavender bag works very well in sewing cotton. Colour can be added in the fan, either to all the pairs at the top of the fan, or the weaver pair which hangs on the left of the fan group.

PATTERN INTERPRETATION

We have a tendency to copy a pricking from a book and make the lace in the same way as the writer whose pricking we are using. All prickings, however, are open to a variety of interpretations. In the first group of patterns in this book we have already seen that there are several ways of making fans, more than one ground and,

in the bookmark, the diamond shapes can be worked in whole or half stitch or as spiders.

If roseground is to be used it must be clearly marked on the pricking before work begins. The wider and more complex the pricking, the greater the combination of interpretations which can be worked. The art is to make a piece of lace which has good contrast between the solid work and the open work, and which has a pleasing appearance.

The following mat is drafted on 2mm paper. The photograph of the complete mat shows a large area of roseground, which is clearly marked on the pricking. The photograph of samples shows some variations in interpretation. There are probably many other combinations which would make an equally attractive mat. There is insufficient space on a page of this book for a full draft of this pricking in 10 squares to 25mm. I have drafted it in sections which can leap-frog over each other in the working.

The advantage of having a square in sections is that with only two corners necessary there is less pricking to do, which is a great advantage in a large project. A pricking can be cut as indicated. The corners will leap-frog over each other to make a square. Sections of the straight lace can be added as required to make an oblong or to increase the size of the original square.

Prickings for a smaller lavender bag.

A pricking open to various interpretations (2mm graph paper).

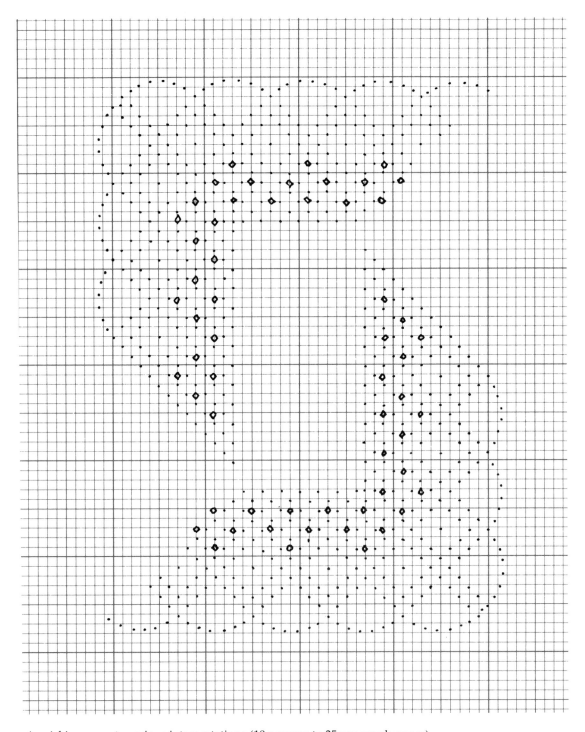

A pricking open to various interpretations (10 squares to 25mm graph paper).

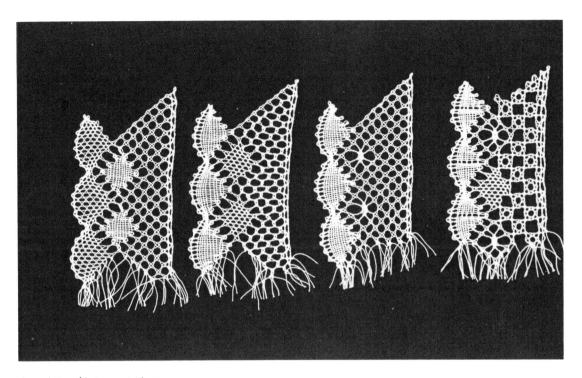

A variety of interpretations.

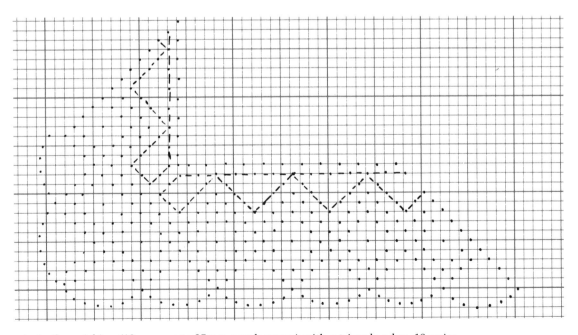

A similar pricking (10 squares to 25mm graph paper) with a triangle edge. 18 pairs.

A complete mat using roseground. I used DMC Retors 30.

A complete mat with a triangle edge. I used Bockens Linen 60.

WHERE DO I BEGIN?

This is a question frequently asked by lacemakers when they become more experienced and discover designs which do not give instructions.

Perhaps it would be more appropriate to ask, 'How am I going to finish off?'

Sewings must be made into the starting line and the ends disposed of as invisibly as possible. Ends can be lost most easily in patches of whole or half stitch. It is best to use a diagonal line down the lace in either direction or a zigzag horizontal line across the lace, incorporating the edges of as much whole stitch or half stitch as possible.

If the lace is to be joined with sewings it is definitely not a good idea to start in a straight line across the lace because each pin-hole will have two pairs running to it and both will have to be sewn in the one hole. An exception to this rule is a trail

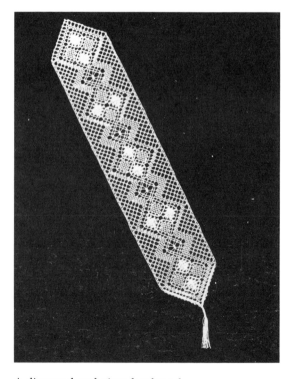

A diamond and gimp bookmark.

94

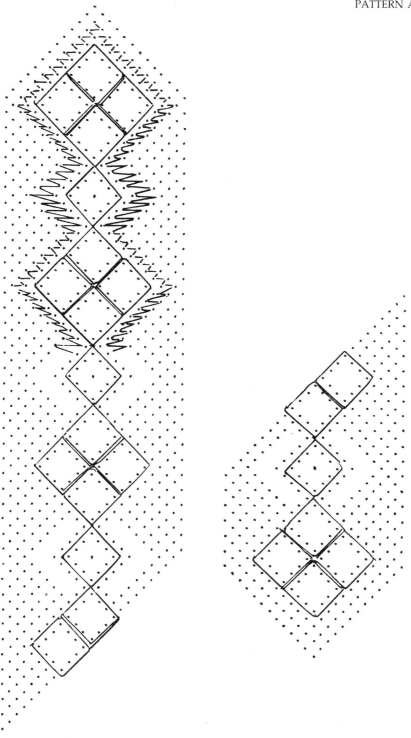

The pricking for a diamond and gimp bookmark. (2mm graph paper). 28 pairs
and 1 gimp pair. I used Mettler 30 and Coton Perle 8.

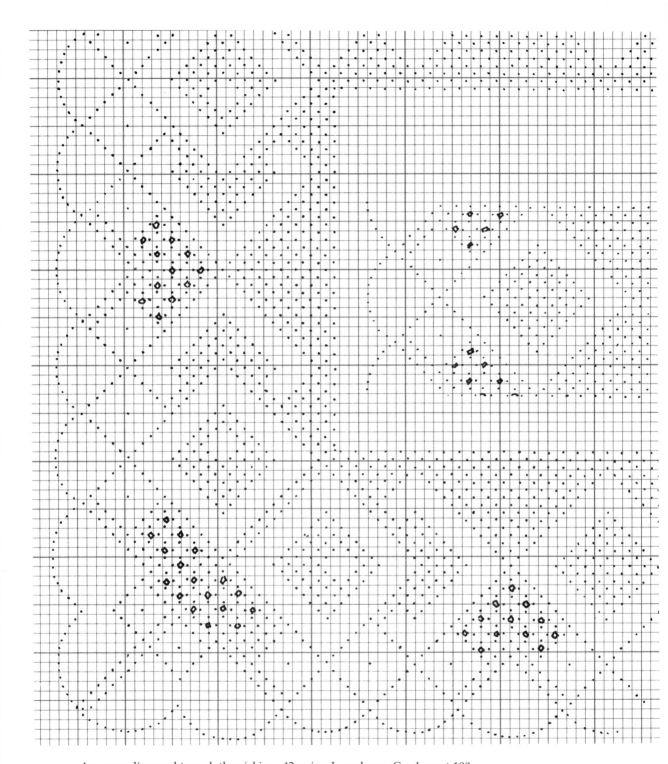

An open diamond tray-cloth pricking. 42 pairs. I used ecru Cordonnet 100.

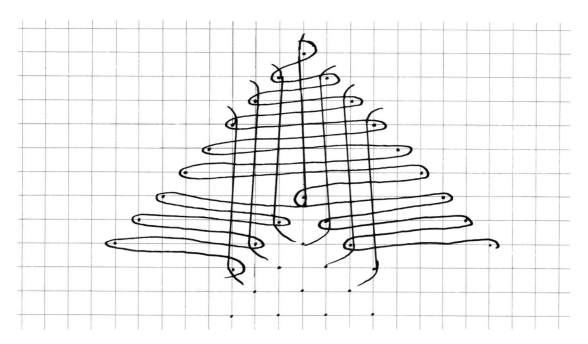

Dividing a trail.

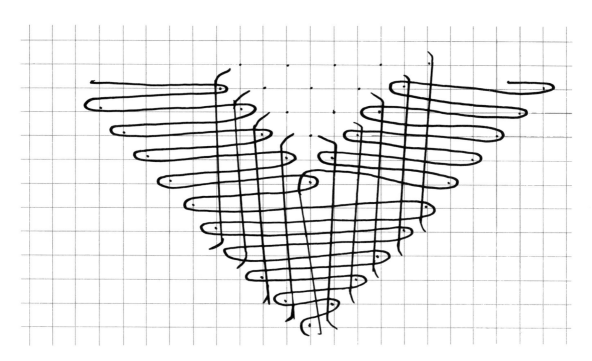

Rejoining a trail.

An open diamond tray-cloth. The pricking had modified fans.

which zigzags the full length of the lace. In this case the trail will have been started with pairs on a line of pins across the trail and individual pairs will be sewn to individual holes.

The patterns in Chapter 4 describe how to start at a footside and ground, how to start a fan and how to start a diamond. For a zigzag start, all three of these may be used, with them all becoming joined together eventually across the width of the lace. Look at the start of the tray-cloth in Chapter 7, Variations on a Theme.

If the pricking is in sections, do not begin work at the top of a section or you will be trying to make sewings across the join in the pricking, always an area of possible inaccuracy at the best of times.

The following patterns are intended to give practice in techniques already learned in Chapter 4.

Dividing a Trail

In the bookmark and tray-cloth design there is an area which starts as a diamond and then the trail is split forming a diamond with a space in the centre.

Work the diamond down to the point at which it is split. An equal number of pins are worked on each side of the diamond. There will be a weaver pair and an odd number of passive pairs. An equal number of passives will enter each trail and the other pair will become the weaver in the other trail.

An open diamond handkerchief. 42 pairs. I used DMC Retors 50.

An open diamond handkerchief. The pricking has modified fans.

For example:
1 weaver pair and 11 passive pairs
will become
1 weaver, 5 passives, 1 weaver, 5 passives.

Look at the diagram and take the weavers through 5 + 1 pairs, put up pin, and cover.

Work the two pairs at the pin to the appropriate edges, bring in a new pair and place the pin. Take the weavers back to the inner edges, place the pin and leave out the pairs to be used in the centre space.

At the point where the trails meet use the two weaver pairs to work to the bottom hole. One pair will become a passive pair and the other pair will be the weavers to complete the diamond. Check if there are an equal number of holes still to be worked on each side of the diamond. If the numbers are equal either pair can become the weavers. If there is a larger number on one side, select the weaver that is going in that direction.

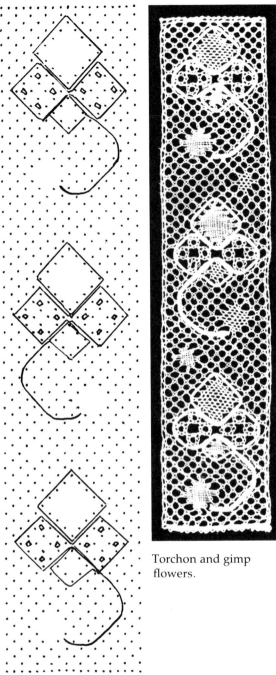

Torchon and gimp flowers.

A pricking for Torchon and gimp flowers. 22 pairs. I used Bockens Linen 90 and Coton Perle 5.

7 Variations on a Theme

In 1987 I was researching Downton lace and came across a set of photographs in a booklet published some years ago by Salisbury Museum. Besides Bucks-type patterns there were many very attractive Torchon designs made at Downton.

I had my first attempts at drafting from a picture at this time. I used 2mm graph paper and worked some samples. I particularly liked the following pattern and thought it would make a good tray-cloth edge. However, Downton lace was worked without corners (the lace was gathered round the corners of handker-chiefs). A gathered corner would be impractical for table linen so I drafted a corner which works quite well. Advice on drafting corners can be found in Chapter 9 (*see* pages 120–122).

Since working the tray-cloth I have modified the shape of the corner fan. The fan is slightly smaller and the pairs are run in the same manner as in the edge fans, giving a stronger, more compact corner.

I liked the diamond and chevron combination and decided to use it in some other ways.

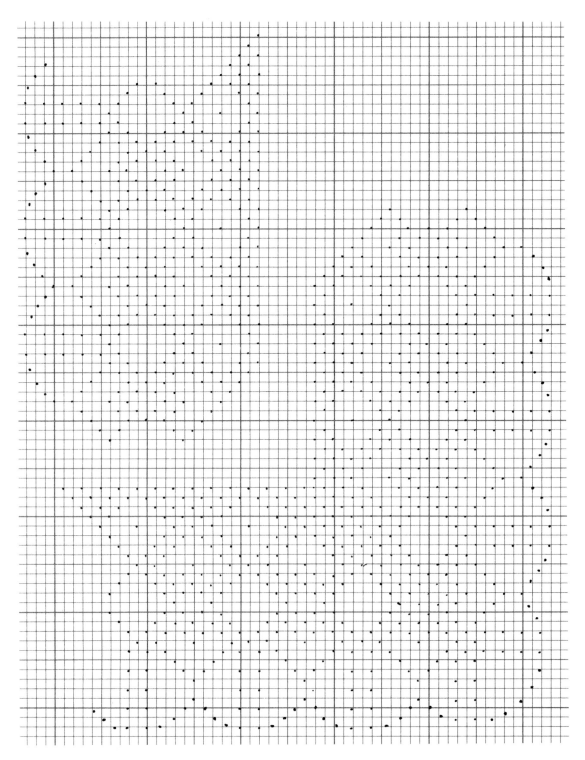

A tray-cloth edging, pricking on 10 squares to 25mm graph paper. 29 pairs. I used DMC Cordonnet 100.

102

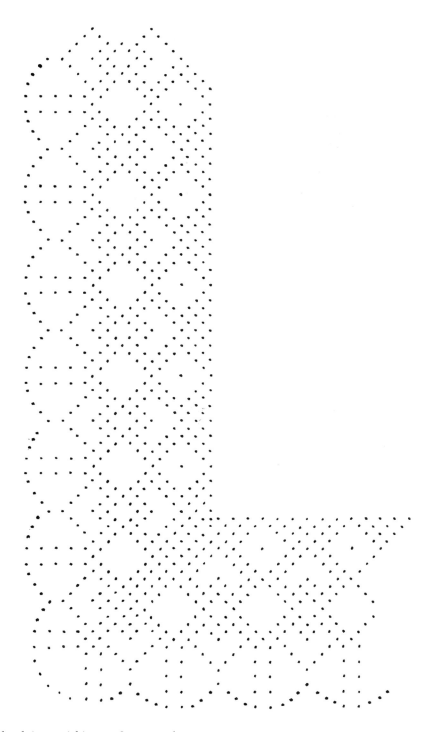

A tray-cloth edging, pricking on 2mm graph paper.

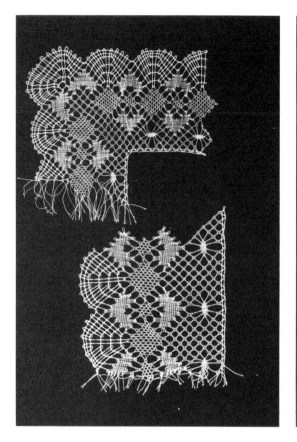

Starting the lace and working the corner.

The complete tray-cloth. (The corner fans are modified on the pricking.)

MATS

Square Mat

In this design the Torchon fan runs across the corner. Work must begin below the corner but is still worked in sections. After the four sections are complete, the fourth corner fan can be worked.

Round Mat

The round grid at the back of this book was drawn for me on a computer. It has 144 dots and by wonderful coincidence this Downton pattern fits perfectly.

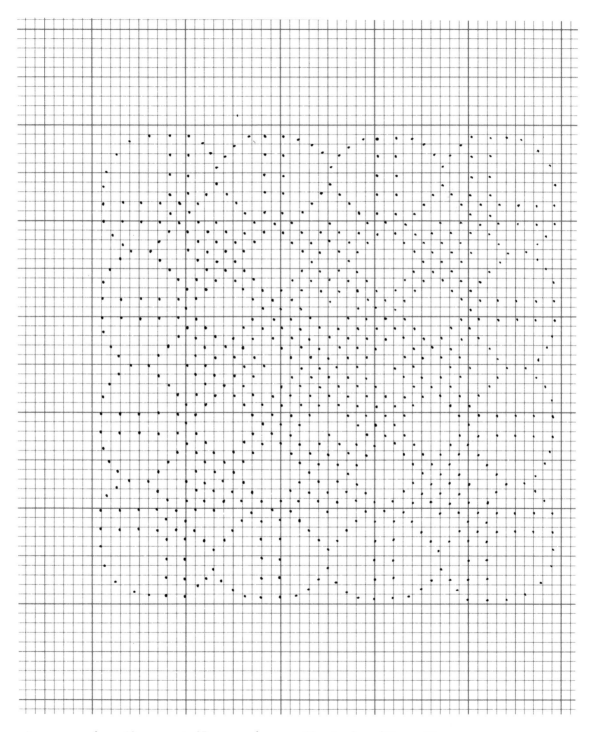

A square made on 10 squares to 25mm graph paper. 19 pairs. I used Tanne 30.

A square made on 2mm graph paper.

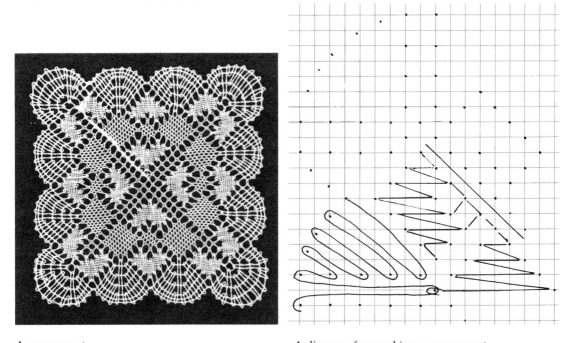

A square mat.

A diagram for working a square mat.

106

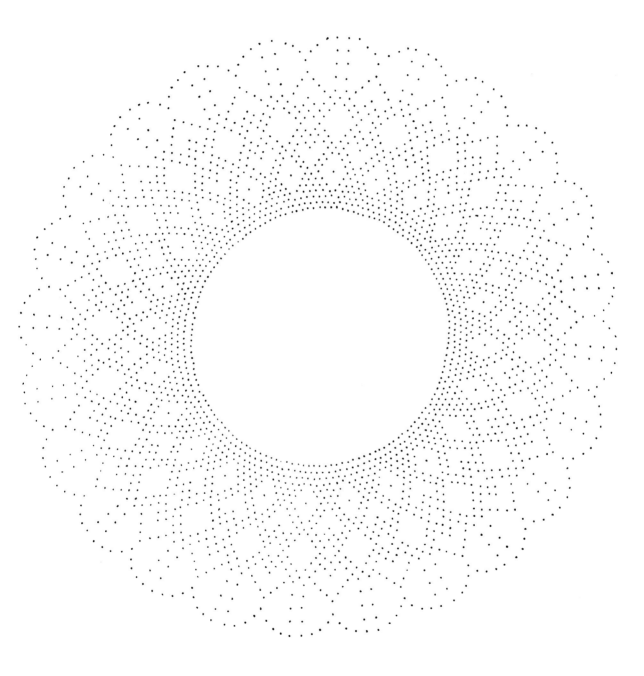

A round mat pricking. 27 pairs. I used DMC Retors 30.

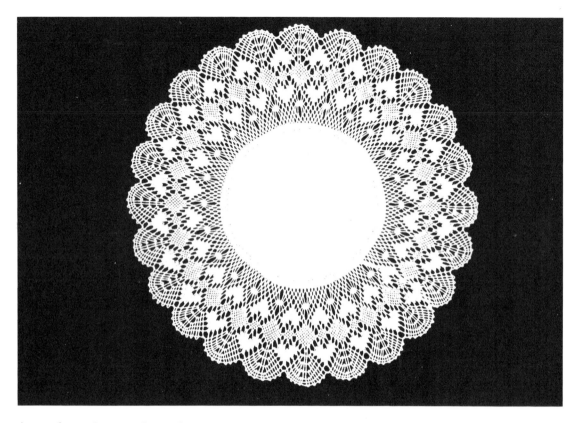

A round mat. Increase the pricking to 125 per cent to gain the original size.

DESIGNING ON A ROUND GRID

Grids are usually worked out on polar graph paper. These are round grids where lines emanate from a central 'pole' and the squares get bigger the further away they are from the middle. There are two problems when working on round grids.

Firstly, the dots become further apart as the spokes of the 'wheel' move further from the centre. The design needs to be heavier at the edge to counteract this effect.

Secondly, there is the problem of designing a pattern with repeats which fit exactly into the grid. My 144 grid is particularly good because 6, 8, 12 and 16 are all factors of 144. It should not be too difficult to design a repeat of one of these sizes. The grid for the round fan-edging mat in Chapter 4 was drawn up on polar graph paper and has 90 dots, and the fan has a repeat of 5 (18 fans × 5 = 90).

Galloon

A galloon is a strip of lace with two shaped edges.

The following galloon was made as a cake frill. It could be used as a belt or, with a finer thread, a garter. You could have your own ideas.

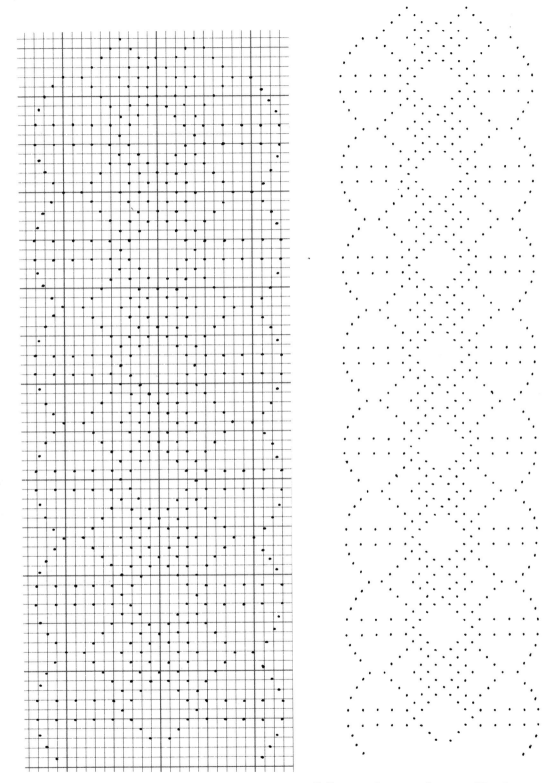

Galloon on 10 squares to 25mm graph paper. 22 pairs. I used Tanne 30.

Galloon on 2mm graph paper. 22 pairs. I used Tanne 30.

109

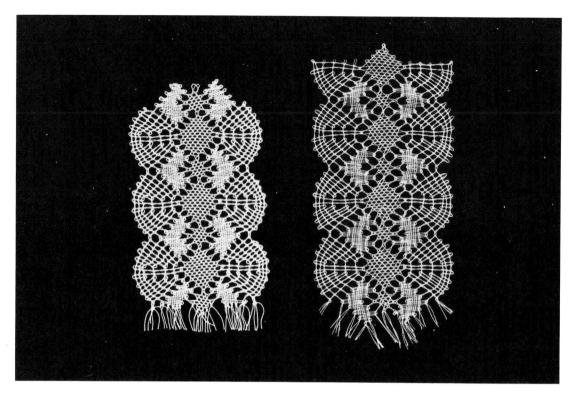

Two sizes of galloon.

ADDING COLOUR

In all these designs the weavers on the Torchon fan edging could be coloured.

On the tray-cloth, round mat and galloon the weavers could be coloured if the diamonds were worked in whole stitch. The chevrons could be worked in half stitch to give a good contrast.

If you are interested in using colour in your lacemaking, be daring. Do not be afraid to experiment.

Try some of the wide range of coloured and textured threads on the market. Try putting colour precisely where you want it by lacemaking techniques (you can confine a colour to the footside by working it with a whole stitch ground), or by using a paint brush and some of the wide range of fabric dyes currently available.

8 Designing Lace

Designing a piece of lace can be a rewarding experience. However, when faced with a blank piece of graph paper, inspiration may evaporate and panic set in.

With the dots and headside already provided, all you need is a sharp pencil and eraser to make some interesting designs of your own. The prickings for the small mats, one with a fan edge, the other a Torchon fan edge, are drafted on 10 squares to 25mm graph paper, the same as that used in Chapter 4. A footside is in place (though this could be moved) and dots fill the remaining area. The corner line is marked and a pattern repeat is indicated.

The pricking for the corner is drafted on 2mm graph paper and has a headside like one of the prickings in Chapter 9. It can be repeated to form a square or cut to the size and shape needed for a particular project. The grid of dots was drawn on a computer and is approximately equivalent to dots which would be produced on 2mm graph paper. It is a good idea to secure a piece of tracing paper over the pricking, so that disasters can be scrapped without ruining the photocopy.

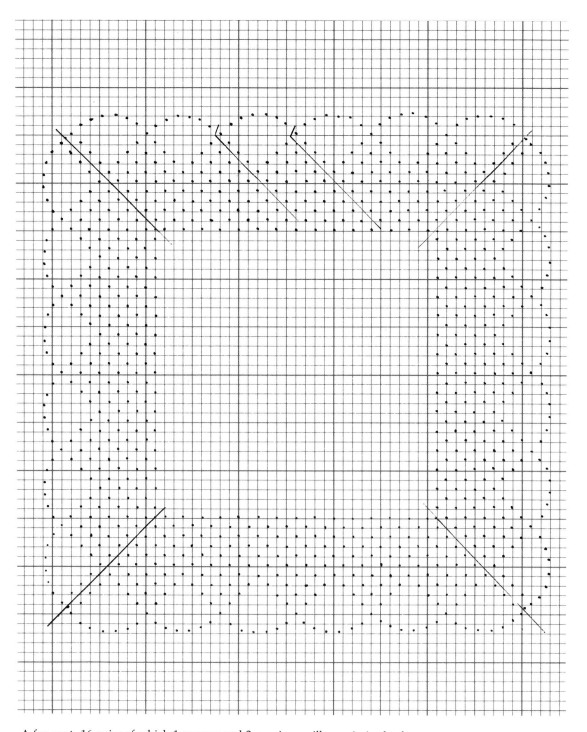

A fan mat. 16 pairs of which 1 weaver and 3 passives will remain in the fan.

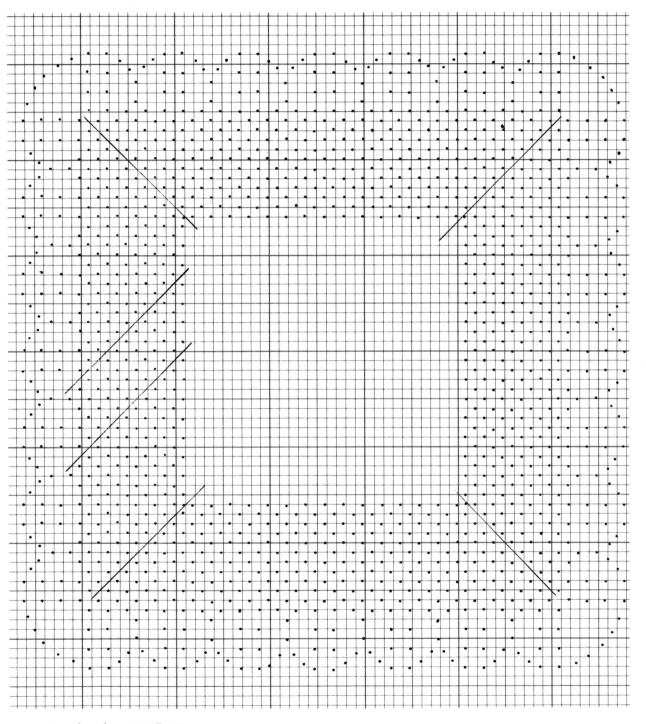

A torchon fan mat. 17 pairs.

Heart-shaped edging on 2mm graph paper. 25 pairs.

Dots approximately equal to 2mm graph paper.

TORCHON MOTIFS

Consider the following:

Torchon ground   One dot.
Roseground   Four dots and spaces between in all directions.
Diamonds   At least three dots diagonally in each direction.
Spiders   At least four dots diagonally in each direction.
Trails   Edges usually at least three diagonal dots apart.
Chevrons   These can be made to appear heart shaped or with longer 'arms' can be placed at four different angles within the edging (point up, point down, point to right or point to left).
Gimps   Used to highlight different elements.

Now plunge in. If you want to put in a diamond, decide how large it is to be and make a pencil line through the dots you wish to use. Similarly a spider and roseground. Use an eraser if you make a mistake. Use a new piece of tracing paper if you make a mess! Work on one side of the pattern. If you are uncertain about placing different motifs, look back in this book or in some other Torchon book. When you are satisfied with your creation, take the plunge and transfer your pencil lines to the pricking on all four sides.

Use a white correction fluid pen to whiten out the dots you do not need, e.g. within diamonds and spiders. Mark in the centres of the spiders in ink. Mark in the roseground in ink. When everything is dry, rub out all the pencil markings. If you wish to keep a record of your designs, photocopy the original or draw out another copy before making the lace.

PATTERN INTERPRETATION

1.   Consider if you are going to add colour, either as weavers or as a gimp.
2.   Consider which stitches you will use to give a balanced texture (whole or half stitch for diamonds, chevrons, fans, etc.)
3.   Now plunge in and have a go.

TORCHON WITH A DIFFERENCE

As I mentioned in Pattern 12 of Chapter 4, vertical and horizontal lines do not occur very often in Torchon designs. Pattern 12 has whole stitch triangles using snatch pins. A mat in Chapter 6 includes smaller half stitch triangles. By using snatch pins on vertical lines and by twisting pairs before they enter horizontal lines it should be possible to design lace with shapes more complex than a triangle. In theory any design which can be drawn on graph paper can be converted to lace!

Fair Isle knitting and various cross stitch embroideries spring to mind. Hardanger embroidery has possibilities, especially the diamond-shaped motifs. Besides Fair Isle there are many knitting designs using one colour and relying on the use of groups of stitches to give changes in texture. Aran designs use this technique.

I include the following samples as possibilities for further development and experimentation. The star shape may well be used with similar 'new' shapes or with more traditional Torchon motifs. I have not included a pricking for the top right design because I do not think the design worth pursuing. If you do not agree you could try drafting it yourself!

Lace from knitting patterns.

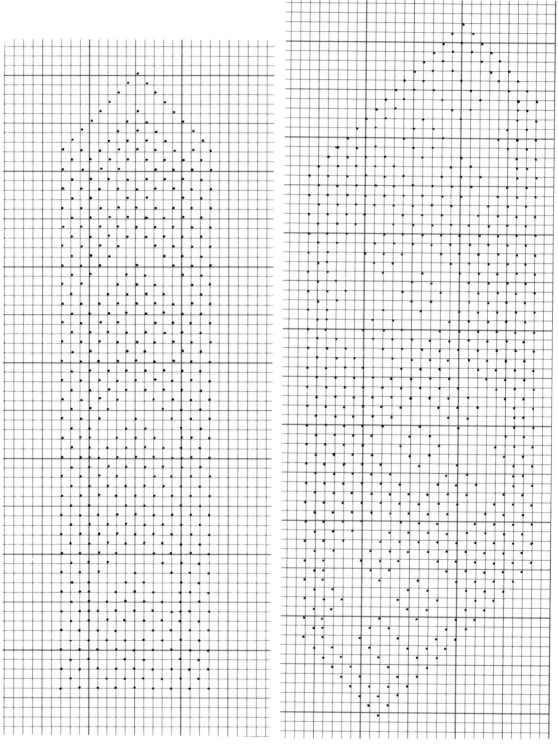

A horizontal chevrons pricking.

A vertical chevron and diamond pricking.

A small star pricking.

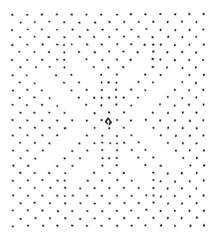

A large star pricking.

9 Drafting from a Picture or Piece of Lace

As you become more hooked on lace-making you will be looking for it everywhere. 'That's a nice piece of lace', has become a catch-phrase in our house. You may see a picture, or come across an edging which appeals to you on a junk stall or in an antique shop.

Make a few notes on a scrap of paper. Count the legs of spiders, count the pin-holes in diamonds, count the pin-holes on edges of fans, count groups of rose-ground and their relative positions, note the stitches used for diamonds and so on. Now get out the graph paper. Remember that the dots are at the intersections of lines on the graph paper, down diagonal lines. This means that horizontally and vertically, alternate intersections are used. Look back to the patterns in Chapter 4.

Plunge in, with a sharp pencil and an eraser at the ready. Do not worry about the head or footside. Try to place the various elements as they are in your notes or picture. Work on only two or three repeats of the design. As it develops, the footside will establish itself.

The inner edge of the headside will be established and if there is a curved outer edge this can be drawn in with a pair of compasses. The number of dots needed to work this edge can be established by drawing a zigzag line across the fan and the holes can then be evenly spaced around the curve.

When you are satisfied, ink in all the dots and pattern markings with a fine felt-tipped pen. When it is completely dry, rub out all the pencil marks. Keep this as your master copy. You are not aiming to make an exact copy, but to produce a representation of something that has appealed to you. You may find you have chosen the wrong size of graph paper and have produced something larger or smaller than the original. This can be rectified if you wish.

The following patterns have been lifted from a travel brochure, a picture postcard sent by a friend from Bruges, and some antique lace in the Museum of Costume in Bath. They have been drafted on 2mm graph paper but the scale could be altered. The corners of these pictures are not very clear so I have designed possible corners, though I am sure there are alternatives.

I have seen the 'tumbling blocks' design worked in a long strip to trim a pillow-case.

DESIGNING CORNERS

As Torchon lace is designed at 45 degrees to the horizontal and vertical, any line running from the footside at top right to the headside at bottom left is a possible mitre line for a corner. By placing a small hand-mirror on any of these lines it is

A fan and chevron design on 2mm graph paper. 20 pairs. I used Tanne 30.

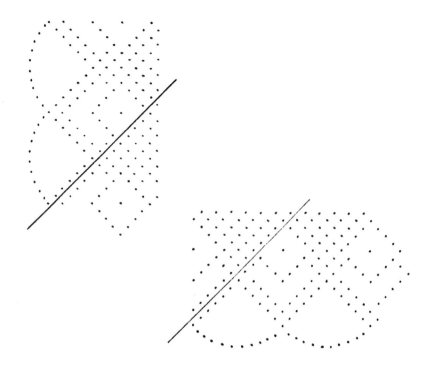

A corner for a fan and chevron design.

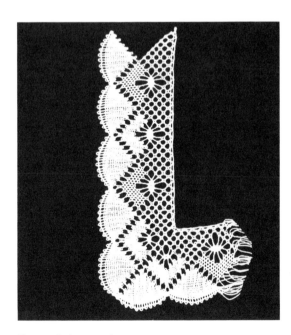

Fan and chevron lace.

possible to see how a corner may look. If the headside is composed of fans, the line most suitable probably runs down the lower edge of the fan.

1.   Trace two lengths of pricking (two repeats will probably be sufficient). You could use lengths of photocopy.
2.   Fold one section along a diagonal line from top left to bottom right. In a fan edge this will probably be along the top edge of a fan.
3.   Turn this piece of pricking at right angles to the other piece and place on a diagonal line running from top right to bottom left.
4.   If the whole repeat of the pattern falls with the repeat of the fan this may form a good corner without further work. *See* the fan-edging pattern on page 55.

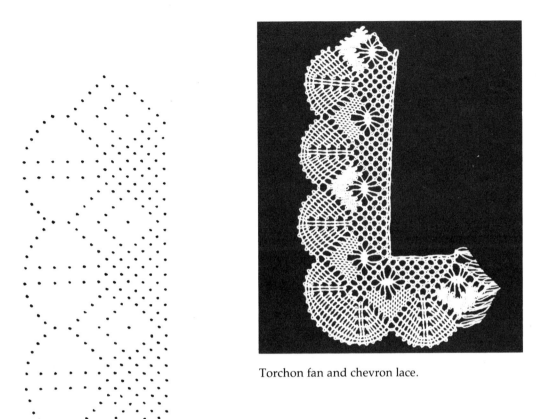

Torchon fan and chevron lace.

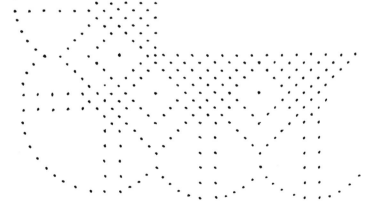

A torchon fan and chevron design on 2mm graph paper. 18 pairs. I used
Mettler 30.

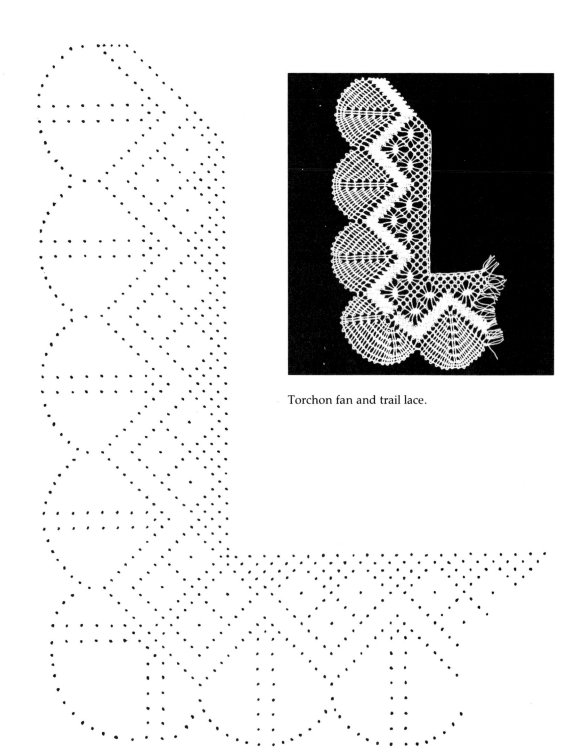

Torchon fan and trail lace.

A torchon fan and trail design on 2mm graph paper. 22 pairs including 5 passive pairs and a weaver pair in the trail. I used DMC Retors 30.

124

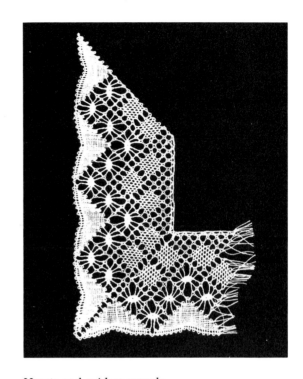

Hearts and spiders sample.

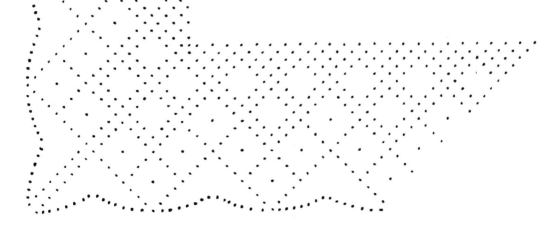

A hearts and spiders design on 2mm graph paper. 25 pairs. I used Bocken
Linen 90 on the sample and Tanne 50 on the completed handkerchief.

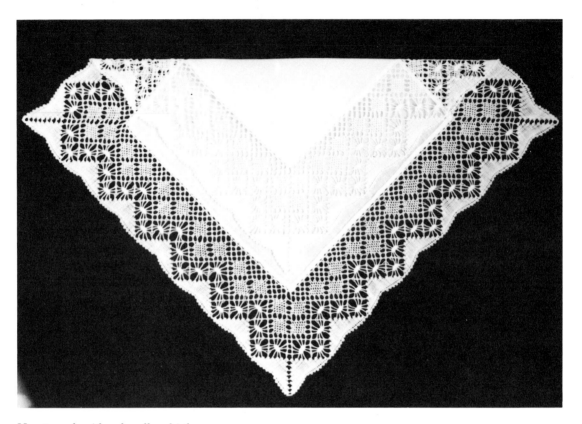

Hearts and spiders handkerchief.

5. The edge of the spider falls below the lower edge of the fan and some alterations must be made. One solution is to make the corner spiders smaller so that they are completed on the corner line. This involves an extra row of ground stitches on one side of the spiders. The centre pin of each spider must also be repositioned.

6. For accuracy the corner should be drafted on graph paper.

7. A similar method can be followed for a Torchon fan design, though it will be necessary to design a corner fan. I have included several examples of Torchon corners and these could be used as guidelines.

126

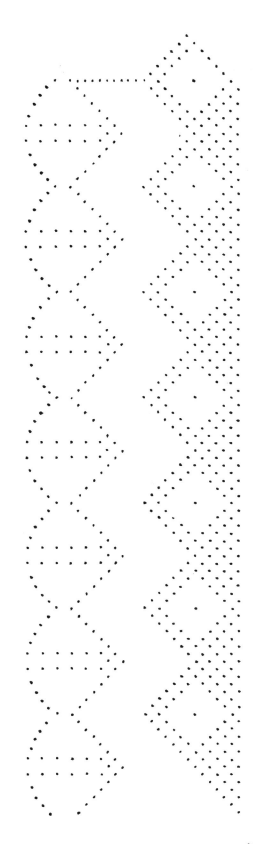

A tumbling blocks design on 2mm graph paper.
28 pairs including 12 passive pairs and 1 weaver
pair in the trail. I used *fil à dentelle* random colour.

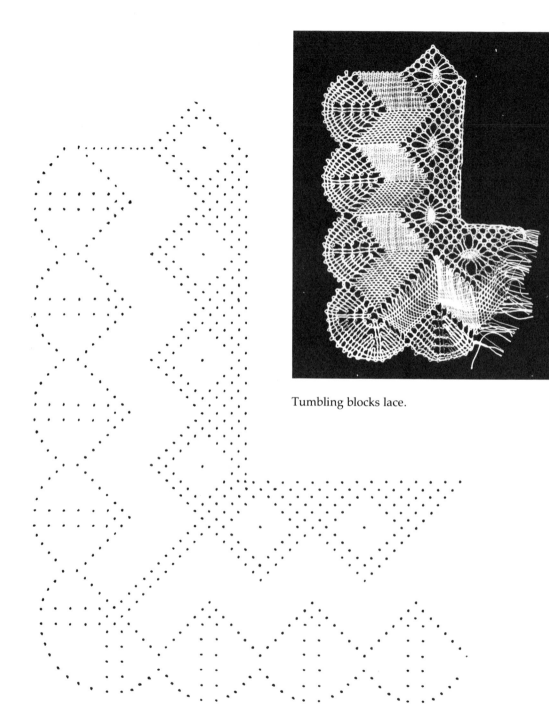

Tumbling blocks lace.

Tumbling blocks corner.

10   Downton Torchon

When I started lacemaking, by learning Torchon, there was much talk about 'coarse' and 'dishcloth'. Although I did not like to say so, I saw no reason why it should not be made of finer thread on a suitably sized grid.

The class visited Salisbury Museum in 1984, and we were all very surprised to see the number of Torchon samples dotted among the Bucks-type Downton patterns. To my delight, most of them were on the same scale as the Downton lace and made with fine thread. Many of the designs were available as an insertion and an edging. They were not very wide and the pricking interpretation added to the variety. The same pricking might have a whole stitch or half stitch trail. The samples of all variations, sewn on long strips of wide, coloured ribbon, which could be rolled for easy storage, were all numbered.

The samples date from early in the century when the old Downton Lace Industry was re-established in 1910 as part of a country-wide revival of hand-made bobbin lace. The Industry had a President, a Secretary and so forth and it worked like this. The customer would choose the design and length required and the Secretary would contact lacemakers who worked for the Industry, to find one who would be willing to do the commission. The Industry supplied the thread and there were master prickings available. Bobbins were also supplied if necessary. There were two prices. The one the maker received and the one the buyer paid. The difference helped to run the Industry and the workers were paid bonuses from any profits. These prices were listed, together with the lace sample number, in a small notebook. There were price increases but not very frequently. Prices were increased in 1934 and again in 1938.

The old Downton Lace Industry ran from 1910–1966. For many years the Secretary was a Miss Glynn. She kept a day book, which is rather like a diary and makes fascinating reading. It includes such entries as:

September 15th 1964.
    Mrs Purkins and Mrs Kemp to tea to get pricking etc. and 6 dozen plain Downton bobbins for a possible lace class. Gave Mrs Kemp a skein of [BKO?] for Mrs Halls order. Gave each of them a dozen really good old bobbins and as many prickings from Mrs Gallington's collection as they liked to take.

November 17th 1964.
    Rec'd from Mrs Kemp 3yds No.237 @ 10/–, 30/–; 2yds No.149 @ 5/9, 1½yds No.103 @ 9/6, 10/7 = £2 14s 4d paid.

January 6th 1966.
    Wrote to Mrs Kemp, Purkins, Kelly and Snelgrove with a view to adjusting prices of lace.

The last entry in the book concerns the presentation of a lace pillow set up with the 'Ace of Spades' to Downton Women's Institute in memory of the Lace Industry which was being disbanded, partly through lack of public interest but mainly I think through Miss Glynn's ill health.

Miss Glynn must have been a very remarkable woman. She was Secretary of the Industry in 1937, if not before, and ran it until 1966. The day-book which I have seen runs from 1957–1966 and there are several entries each week. She was an accomplished lacemaker herself and besides running the Industry gave lessons to others including Industry lacemakers and students of Salisbury College of Arts which was then in New Street, just along the road from her house in Crane Street. I have been told that she was also involved with the Netley Marsh Glove Industry, just over the county border in Hampshire.

I had the Downton Torchon tray-cloth from Chapter 7, 'Variations on a Theme', (*see* pages 102–104) with me when I went to a Downton Lace Day at Salisbury Museum in 1989. I found myself sitting next to Mrs Joyce Yates of Totton near Southampton making the same pattern. She was using a copy of a Downton original and her lace was much narrower than mine. Lacemakers' generosity never ceases to amaze me. Joyce got out her scissors and cut off a section of her pricking so that I could have it as a comparison.

I have since discovered a way of drafting Downton Torchon which comes out slightly smaller than the original. It can be done by taking a sheet of 2mm graph paper and turning it through 45 degrees so that the printed lines of the graph paper run diagonally in both directions. The drafting is done as before, but the resulting pricking will run diagonally across the sheet. This means that the pricking must start well down the page on one side of the sheet to get a good length of pricking. I have drafted the following pricking from the photograph which I have mentioned in 'Variations on a

Theme' (*see* page 101). They are in two sizes; the larger on 2mm paper by the usual method and the smaller with the paper turned through 45 degrees. I have drafted with the footside on the left because that was the Downton way. The pricking could be turned upside down to put the footside on the right if you do not feel you can cope with a left-hand footside. However some of the pieces are for insertions and we have always coped with a left footside in an insertion.

Changing Size by Photocopy

It can be very trying on the eyes to draft on a smaller size than 2mm graph paper. An alternative would be to use the services of a photocopier. You can either 'make it small' (reduce) or decide precisely what you want.

The arithmetic is easier if worked in millimetres. You need to know the length or width of the pricking and the length or width you would like it to be.

$$\frac{\text{size you want}}{\text{size it is}} \times 100 = \text{percentage increase or decrease}$$

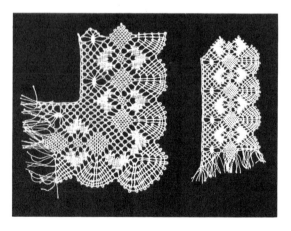

A photograph of both sizes.

130

The small size. I used Retors 50.

The large size from Chapter 7, Variations on a Theme.

Small size. 20 pairs. I used Retors 50.

A photograph of both sizes.

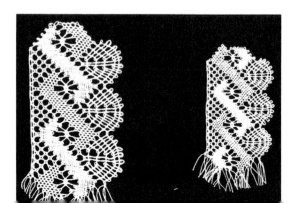

Large size. 20 pairs. I used Mettler 30.

132

Small size. 20 pairs. I used Fresia Linen 140.

A photograph of both sizes.

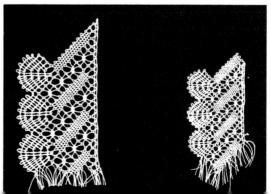

Large size. 20 pairs. I used Retors 30.

Small size.

Large size. I used Tanne 50 (too fine).

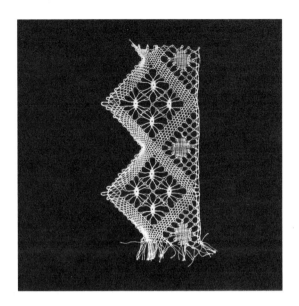

A photograph of the large size.

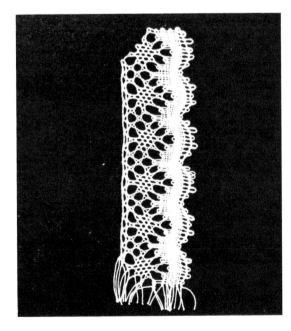

A photograph of the small size.

Large size. 14 pairs. I
used sewing cotton.

Small size.

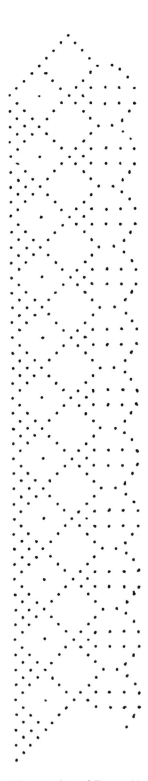

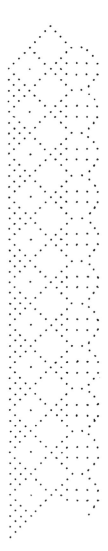

Small size. I used Pipers Silk 130/3.

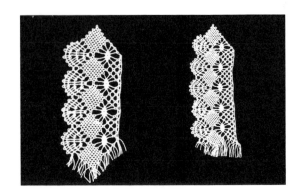

Large size. 17 pairs. I used Tanne 30.

A photograph of both sizes.

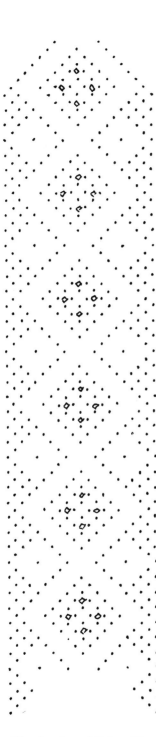

Large size. 26 pairs. I used Retors 30.
(There are 10 pairs in the trail before it
divides.)

Small size.

A photograph of the large size.

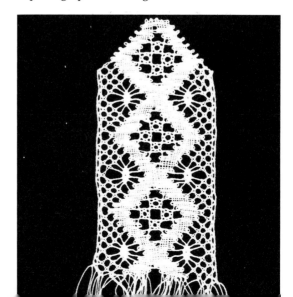

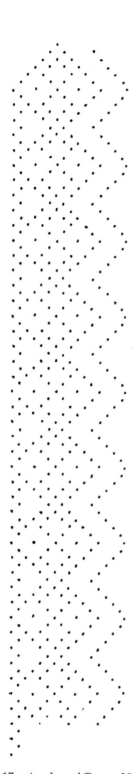

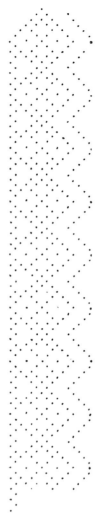

Small size.

A photograph of the large size.

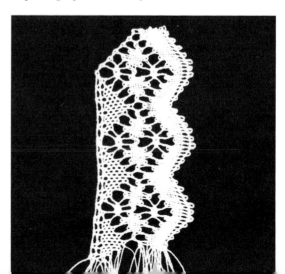

Large size. 17 pairs. I used Tanne 30.

138

Small size.

A photograph of the large size.

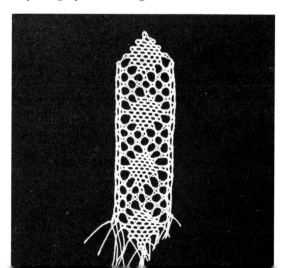

Large size. 12 pairs. I used sewing cotton.

Small size. I used Egyptian cotton 120.

A photograph of both sizes.

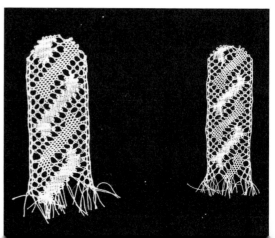

Large size. 18 pairs. I used sewing cotton.

140

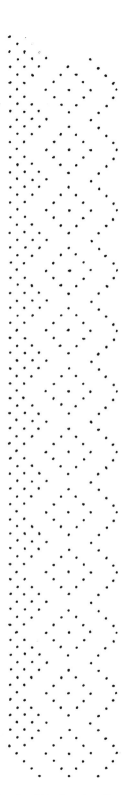

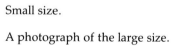

Small size.

A photograph of the large size.

Large size. 18 pairs (7 in head trail and 5 in inner trail). I used sewing cotton.

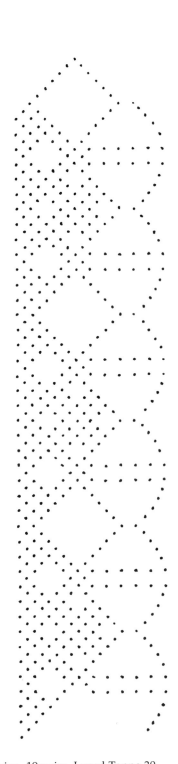

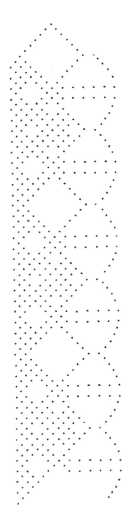

Small size.

A photograph of the large size.

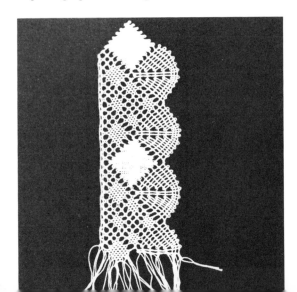

Large size. 19 pairs. I used Tanne 30.

142

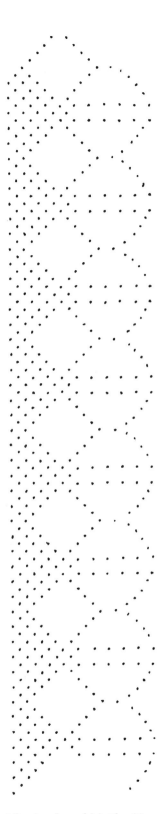

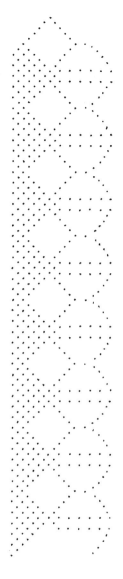

Small size.

A photograph of the large size.

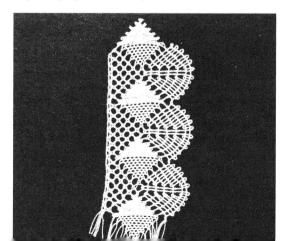

Large size. 17 pairs. I used Mettler 30.

Large size. 25 pairs would be needed.   Small size.

11 Cake Frills and Garters

Although this may seem a strange combination, both require a length of lace – although the cake frill need not necessarily be gathered.

Many people find cake icing a daunting task. They find it especially difficult to make a smooth finish on the sides of the cake. A cake frill can cover a multitude of sins. A frill or band of lace can be very attractive, either coloured lace with white icing showing through, or white or coloured lace mounted on coloured ribbon. The choice of colour can be geared to the occasion.

All lacemakers at some time get called upon to make a bridal garter and although Bucks point lace is finer, there is no reason why it should not be made of Torchon lace. The traditional colours are white and blue.

Cake frills and garters can be constructed in a variety of ways. If the lace is to be gathered, an elaborate centre design will be lost in the gathers and consequently is a waste of time. Ungathered lace will need a firm thread which will produce a crisp finish, while gathered lace will need a more delicate thread which gathers well but still holds its shape.

METHOD 1

A length of galloon lace (both edges shaped) may be worked. For a cake frill this may be mounted on ribbon. For a garter the lace may be attached to a shirring strip of elastic. This is available in varying widths from haberdashery departments. To follow this method, make the required length of lace, one and a half times the measurement of the bride's leg and join the end to the beginning by sewings or a simple seam. Take the required length of elastic and join the ends. Do not make a garter that is too tight. Put the completed lace around something fairly rigid, wrong side towards you. I have successfully used the blocks from a block pillow. Stretch the elastic so that it is on the centre portion of the lace. Stitch it in position through the lace on both edges, using small stitches, and making sure you do not attach it to your base. Release the garter from the base and turn it right side out. The centre elasticated area may be trimmed at intervals with small bows, pearl beads etc., or with a larger trimming at one spot on the garter.

METHOD 2

A length of galloon lace with eyelet holes through the centre may be used. Suitably coloured ribbon may be woven through the eyelets.

For a cake frill the lace may be gathered up by the ribbon or left flat. In either case the ribbon and lace must be sewn together at each end of the frill to stop the ribbon coming unthreaded. The frill can be placed around the cake and the ends joined with pins. Count the number of pins you

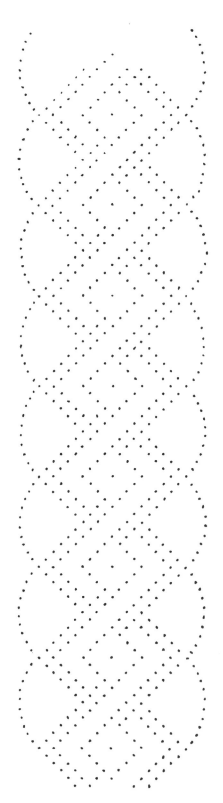

A fan and trail design on 2mm graph paper. 26 pairs. I used Coats Mez Garn.

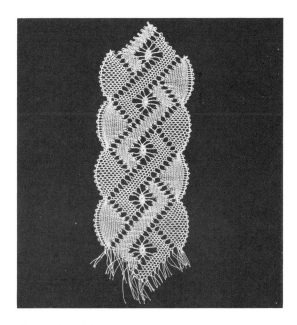

Fan and trail lace.

use and remove the same number before cutting the cake.

For a garter the lace must be made into a continuous band. This can be threaded with a length of elastic and a length of ribbon to cover the elastic. The elasticated area can be decorated as before but the trimmings should be sewn to the ribbon. Sewing them on to the elastic could impede the garter's ability to stretch freely.

METHOD 3

Two lengths of lace edgings can be worked. For the cake frill they can be gathered on each side of a suitable ribbon. The ribbon can be trimmed with suitable beads, bows etc. and the whole pinned around the cake. For a garter use a double layer of ribbon through which to pass the elastic.

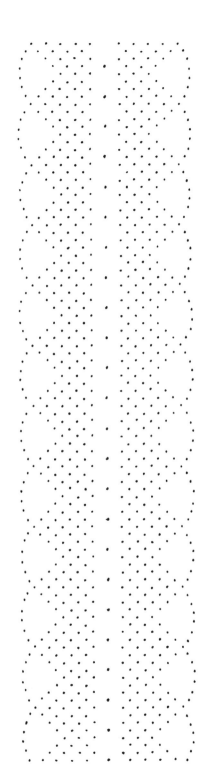

A fan design. 24 pairs. I used Pipers 60/3 silk. (The eyelets can be formed with half stitch, pin, half stitch or whole stitch, pin, whole stitch.)

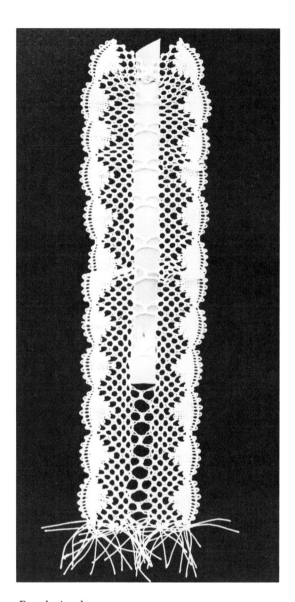

Fan design lace.

In methods 2 and 3, when knicker elastic is being used, make sure that the two ends are overlapped and the join made very secure.

The galloon variation in Chapter 7 (*see* pages 109–110) would fit equally well into this chapter.

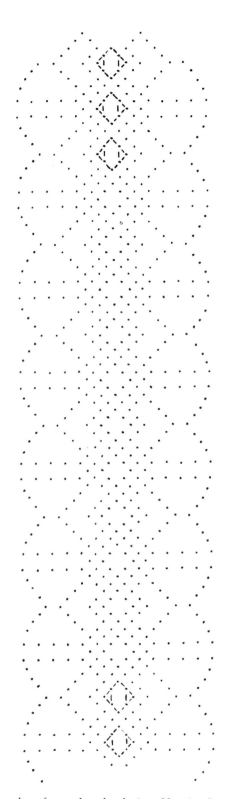

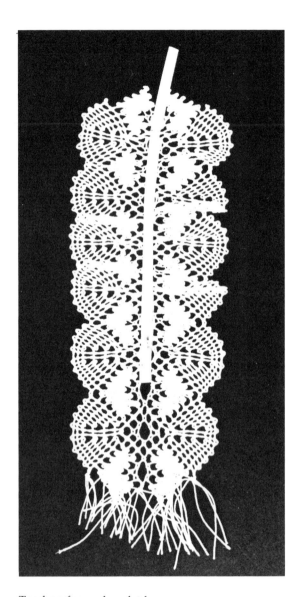

Torchon fan and eyelet lace.

A torchon fan and eyelet design. 22 pairs. I used Pipers 60/3 silk. (The eyelets are worked in Honeycomb stitch.)

148

12 Christmas Lace

DECORATIONS

Lace can be used in a variety of ways for decorations, as simple or elaborate as your imagination, skill and time allows. If you hoard anything decorative which comes your way, you may not need to buy anything in order to carry out these ideas.

Baubles

I do not like odd samples of lace that are pushed away and never see the light of day. There are, however, times when a test piece is necessary to avoid wasting thread on a pricking for which it is not suitable. You may also like to experiment with threads of different types and all these pieces may well be suitable for a Christmas tree decoration or to add to an old bauble and give it a new lease of life.

There is now quite a wide variety of sparkling metallic-type thread available with which to experiment. Also available are polystyrene or compressed paper balls and a wide variety of ribbons. Put these together in your own way and you will have a uniquely dressed tree.

Ribbons and lace can be attached to polystyrene balls with pins using the pin heads as part of the design. If the bauble is such that pins cannot be used, then there are a wide variety of glues available. Read the small print on the packet because some varieties will dissolve certain materials. In both of these methods, the end of the lace from which the bobbins were cut can be fixed under the neater starting end.

The simplest idea would probably be a braid comprising two footsides joined with whole stitch, pin, whole stitch or half stitch, pin, half stitch. By using threads of different colours you will learn the paths they take through the work and at the same time add a seasonal touch. The resulting eyelet strip can be threaded with ribbon and the whole piece attached around a ball or bauble of some kind.

Fringing can be made with three footside pairs and one other pair which could be of a contrasting colour. Work the whole piece in whole stitch and twist following the number sequence in the diagram. The depth of fringe is a matter of choice. A more elaborate and wider footside could be used and the fringe can be left in the form of loops or cut.

I have included the pricking for patterns 2, 3 and 4 of Chapter 4, drafted on 2mm graph paper. These can make attractive additions to baubles and colour can again be used as desired.

Angels

Small angels can be made by topping a compressed paper cone with a compressed ball or suitably sized bauble. The cone can be covered with coloured felt or fabric and then draped with lace. Silver wing shapes can be added. If you are artistic you can give the angel a face.

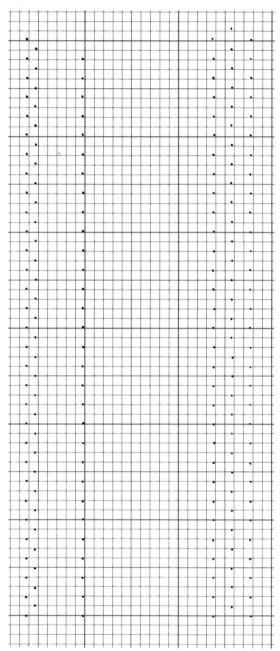

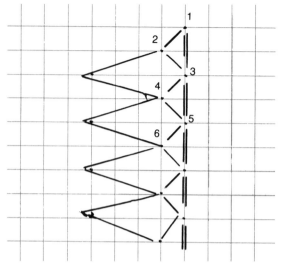

The order for working a fringe.

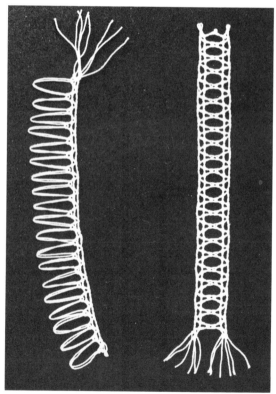

Left; a pricking for footside eyelets. 6 pairs.
I used Cordonnet 100.

Right; a pricking for a fringe. 4 pairs. I used
Cordonnet 100.

Fringe and eyelet lace.

Baubles and a small angel trimmed with lace.

A pricking for a ground strip and diamond strip on 2mm graph paper.

Larger Angels

If you already have a Christmas 'angel' or 'fairy', it may well be that her dress could do with a face-lift. This can again be done with bits and pieces or a specially designed piece. A muslin dress could be

A national costume angel.

151

A pricking for an angel's dress. Photocopy to 125 per cent to gain the original size. 38 pairs. I used Retors 50 and silver gimp.

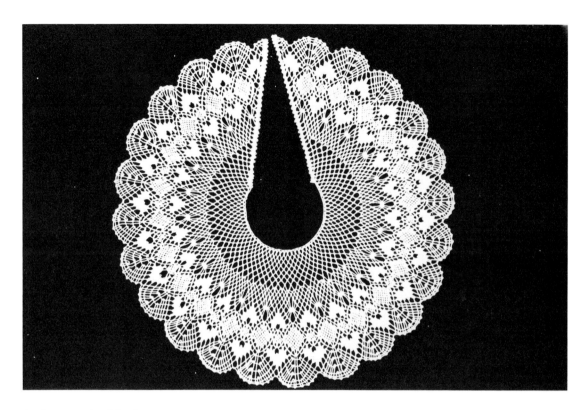

A photograph of flat lace.

washed, starched and trimmed with an edging, or lengths of overlapped edgings could be joined to give the depth of the whole dress.

My angel was originally a national costume doll from a junk stall. She has a semi-circle of lace seamed down the back and draped over a piece of green net to show the pattern elements. Silver wings can be added.

My angel, with dress and wings combined, came out of conversations in class. Sue Gatehouse, who is employed in a Dorset school, suggested that children make complete angels by cutting into a circle of paper. She brought a sample for us to see. By fiddling with paper and then net, I came up with a shape which I

The lace on the angel. There is no gimp in this lace.

subsequently worked in lace. The lace design and circle are the same one used for the mat in Chapter 7, but with a smaller hole in the middle.

Pairs for the lace are sewn into a narrow braid at one end. The braid pairs form a footside at the waist of the dress and then form another braid at the completion of the piece into which the pairs are sewn. A diagonal cross of stiff wire is needed to hold the wings in shape. The edges of the wings are glued to the top two arms of the cross. The arm holding the left wing passes on top of the skirt at the right and vice versa.

Hanging Pairs into a Braid

1. Hang a pair on a support pin to the left of the braid.
2. Take the weavers in the braid through the pair hung on the support pin and place pin.
3. Work back through this pair and the others in the braid.
4. Remove the support pin and leave the new pair against the pin.
5. The pairs hung into the braid will be used to work the lace in the dress.
6. When the dress is complete the pairs which have made the dress will be worked into another braid.

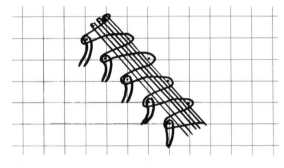

Hanging pairs into a braid.

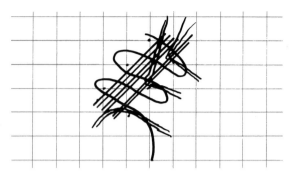

Finishing lace into a braid.

Sewing Pairs into a Braid

1. Take the weavers through the braid and through the appropriate pair to be taken in.
2. Place the pin and tension the weavers and braid pairs.
3. Work whole stitch with the newly taken-in pair and the first passive pair.
4. Take the weavers across the passives to the outer edge and place pin.
5. Throw the taken-in pair to the back of the work.
6. Bring the weavers back to the inner edge and take in another pair in the same manner.
7. The thrown-out pairs can be cut off close to the braid after the work is complete.

SMALL GIFTS

When giving away your precious lace it is important that the recipient appreciates how much time you have taken to work a very small gift.

Bookmarks

These can be made in a variety of sizes and presented in plastic sleeves which

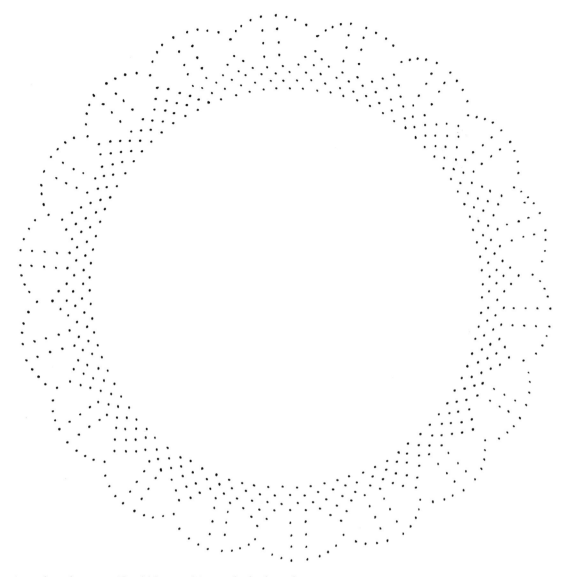

A torchon fan mat. (Could be used instead of a fan edging mat.)

will help to preserve their good looks. They can be backed with ribbon if desired.

I was once criticized in a Women's Institute show for making a bookmark which was too small. 'It should run the length of the page.' I have included my retaliation in Chapter 6. It is too long for this book, and to work it the pricking would have to be joined!

Gift tokens are often frowned on with connotations of laziness on the part of the giver. However, I think a book token and a bookmark would make a very acceptable gift.

Small Mats and Handkerchiefs

A wide variety of mats and handkerchiefs can be worked from the prickings already supplied. By adding or removing repeats of the pricking any desired shape can be achieved.

Round mats can be used as caps for preserves. Hold them in place with an elastic band and then trim with a narrow ribbon and possibly a small flower. My example is a 'honey jar' of marmalade trimmed with a white lace mat, green ribbon and a shaded orange rose (from a box of chocolates) which goes beautifully with the marmalade colour. The mat can be used for its true purpose when the preserve has been consumed, and serve as a lasting memory.

Pot-Pourri and Lavender

All things scented are very fashionable at the moment. Gift shops and herbalists are full of expensive containers and wrappings of a wide variety of mixtures, or the mixtures can be purchased by weight and used as desired. If you are keen you can make your own scented concoction. There are many old recipes available. I do not make my own pot-pourri but I do dry my own lavender.

I have placed my ready-mixed pot-pourri in another honey jar topped with a round mat and trimmed as before. The lace is a fan edging with green sparkling weavers mounted with small running stitches on to green net which will allow the perfume through. Again the rose is from a chocolate box.

Lavender Bags

I have already included a design for a fairly elaborate bag. A simpler idea would be a round, square or heart-shaped bag edged with lace.

Pincushions

Pincushions trimmed with lace make very acceptable gifts. Heart shapes are traditional and these can be stuffed with emery, bran or sheep's wool. The lace can be attached by sewing, although commercially it often seems to be attached by pins or pins on which small beads are threaded, and these form part of the design. The lace can be gathered by putting a draw-thread in the footside. A slightly ruffled effect can be achieved by working around a round pricking once, twice or more to achieve the required length before attaching it to the straight edge.

Ear-rings

Small pieces of lace can be made and attached to hooks for pierced ears. They should swing freely from the hook because their movement adds to their interest. They may be of white or coloured thread and beads may be added for weight or as part of the design. If designing lace ear-rings, take note of the length available from earlobe to shoulder. Some necks are not as long as one might imagine.

The two designs included are the end portions of pattern 3 in Chapter 4 (*see* pages 53 and 54). The lower edges have been finished as described in that pattern, until five pairs are accumulated, when they have been thrown back over the work as described in pattern 10, the Gimp and Roseground Bookmark (*see* page 70). The resulting tassel has been threaded through a large-holed bead and the tassel trimmed. The resulting lace has been stiffened and moulded over a curve, in this case a broad pen.

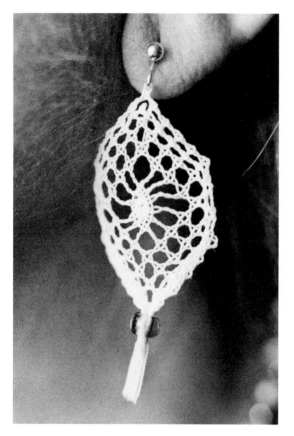

Torchon ear-rings kindly modelled by Marjorie Beal.

If you do not wish to stiffen your lace but are worried about the finishing off, there is a product called 'Fray Check' made by Newey and available in their haberdashery displays. Threads can be cut close and treated with this liquid and this should be made very secure.

Stiffening Lace

Lace can be stiffened while it is still pinned on the pillow, by using spray starch or hairspray, or a spray manufactured for stiffening blinds. If this is planned, the pricking should be covered, before work starts, with transparent book film or a sheet of cling film or plastic, which will not be dissolved by the substance which is used for spraying. This will avoid any colour or marking from the pricking passing to the lace while it is damp from the spray. The resulting lace will be well shaped and flat, but not very stiff.

To shape lace and to make it stiffer it must be removed from the pillow before treatment. Before beginning any treatment make sure that any holes which will be needed in the finishing are preserved. With ear-rings, place pins in the holes where the hooks will go.

Sugar Stiffening This stiffening makes a rigid fabric with threads of thickened appearance. It is a method which often appears in articles on crochet. Stiff, moulded crochet baskets can be made to hold sweets or dried flowers and look very attractive. There is no reason why lace baskets cannot be made in the same way.

However, sugar does absorb dampness in the atmosphere so, although I have used it successfully with the half stitch diamond-shaped ear-rings, it would probably be unwise to wear them outside on a damp day. The result might be very sticky!

The recipes say the following: 'Dissolve 2 tablespoons of sugar in 1 tablespoon of water and boil, but do not allow to caramelize. Cool slightly and dip in the lace. Place over a mould to dry.' This quantity would be lost in a saucepan but I have made it successfully in a microwave by heating in a small glass bowl for ten seconds at a time until a gluey colourless consistency is obtained. The sugar should dissolve before boiling begins. Remember that the resulting 'glue' is extremely hot. You are on the way to making toffee. Allow it to cool naturally before dipping in the lace. Allow it to drain well, before hanging to dry. I did not put the tassel in the solution and allowed it to drain towards the point before hanging it on a needle projecting from a well-scrubbed and cling-film-covered potato resting in a beaker. You will no doubt think of something less improbable.

When all the stickiness has gone but before it becomes rigid, the ear-ring can be moulded to the desired shape.

Blind Stiffening The spider ear-rings have been stiffened with a spray for stiffening blinds. The result moulds well but is not rigid. There are many such products available in department stores which deal in curtain fabric. There are also 'paint on' plastic stiffeners which give a more rigid finish. I have also used an American product which advises squeezing the lace well with the product. This was not a good idea because it was difficult to pull the lace back into shape before moulding it.

Moulding requires some thought. I made the square mat from 'Variations on a Theme' (*see* pages 104–106) and planned to mould it over a curved stainless steel dish. The result looked like a piece of lace with slightly raised corners and nowhere near as artistic as the mould. Not wanting to waste the lace, I dampened it and put it over a jam jar, holding it in place with an elastic band. The result is reminiscent of the type of tin ashtray one used to see screwed down in cinema foyers. The fans show how difficult it was to pull into shape when it had been squeezed.

Other Ideas

My ideas for small gifts so far have been expensive only in time spent in the making.

With some financial outlay lace can be mounted under paperweights or in small frames, or possibly used as an edging for some suitable picture. Lace-edged pictures together with pot-pourri seem very fashionable at the moment. The lace can first be laid on suitably coloured fabric before the mounting. There are many sticky-backed felt-finished products available for mounting crafts and while these are good in their place, if you are making something that might be classed as an heirloom it is worth spending money on something of quality to match the work-

A variety of small gifts.

manship. If you or your friends are hoarders you may well find a suitable piece of silk or velvet among these collections. Small areas of coloured cotton can be purchased in the form of handkerchiefs. This is cheaper than buying a whole width of fabric sold by the metre. There are some other thoughts on mounting in Chapter 5.

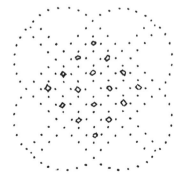

A fan roseground mat on 2mm graph paper. 12 pairs. I used Retors 30.

159

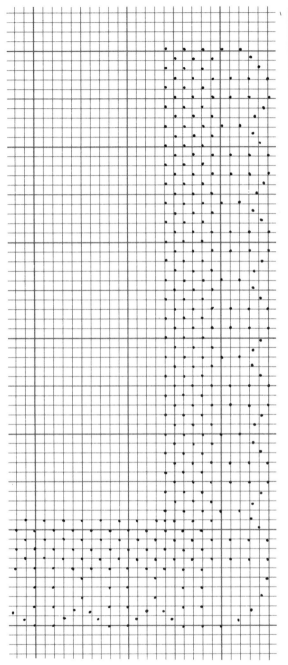

Torchon fan lace used in picture mounting.

A pricking for Torchon fan edging used to frame a photograph. 11 pairs. I used Tanne 30.

13 Odds and Ends

If you have become hooked on lacemaking you will need to keep a record of your work for future reference. It is a good idea to mark prickings with the number of pairs required and the thread or threads which you used and possibly the length of thread which you wound on the bobbin. You may think that you will remember but this is not necessarily so. As your collection of threads grows so may the difficulties. After all, white thread looks like white thread! Try to keep thread labels attached to the thread.

The actual pieces of lace can be stored in a loose-leaf file in transparent plastic sleeves, or in a photo album which includes transparent sheets which normally cover the photographs. If you are giving a piece of lace away you can record it by photography or more easily by photocopying it. Lace can be photocopied very well if placed on a dark backing.

Good lace and thread should be stored in an acid-free environment. It is possible to purchase acid-free tissue paper and boxes. Blue tissue paper used to be the traditional colour for storing linen along with the 'washing blue' used to keep the linen white but which often it made grey.

Lace should not be stored with starch in it. It should be rolled rather than folded as folds, in time, will crack the threads. Dampness can lead to the formation of mould. Light can weaken fabrics, hence the dim light in museums which have fabric collections. Silk and wool can be attacked by moths.

On the other hand, if you make lace, use it or give it to somebody who will appreciate it and use it.

FINDING A LACE TEACHER

It is certainly more stimulating and exciting to learn to make lace when in a group with others. If you are keen to make lace and feel you need a teacher there are a number of different avenues you can explore.

Enquire about classes at your local education authority or arts centre.

Contacting such bodies as the Women's Institute or Townswomen's Guild can be a starting-point in the UK. Your local library may hold a list of useful addresses.

In Britain, the Lace Guild can be contacted at 'The Hollies', 53 Audnam, Stourbridge, West Midlands, DY8 4AE. If you enclose a stamped addressed envelope they will send you the address of a teacher in your area. However, you do not need to belong to the Lace Guild.

Besides lace classes there are also a number of Lace Groups in the UK. They usually meet less frequently than a class but gather periodically to make lace, listen to a speaker and talk over problems.

Membership of the Lace Guild (address above) or the Lacemakers Circle, 49 Wardwick, Derby, DE1 1HU, will each bring you four newsletters a year which include prickings and instructions for a wide variety of laces of varying complexity. They also include long lists of suppliers, news of courses – sometimes residential – in a variety of laces, and lace days.

WHAT IS A LACE DAY?

A lace day is an event which lacemakers can attend and where they can meet like-minded enthusiasts. Suppliers are in attendance and it is a good idea to decide how much you can afford before you get carried away. You do save postage! Often a snack lunch is included in the cost. Frequently, supplies can be bought in the morning and there will be a speaker on a lace topic in the afternoon. A lace suppliers' fair is a similar event, but there will be no speaker, and refreshments will be optional and extra to the entrance fee.

Residential courses are run by the Women's Institute at Denman College in Oxfordshire. They include at least one on lace in their yearly schedule. Local authority colleges like Dillington in Somerset and Lackham in Wiltshire hold occasional courses. The British College of Lace holds courses throughout the year. Information can be obtained from Springetts, 21, Hillmorton Road, Rugby, Warwickshire, CV22 5DF.

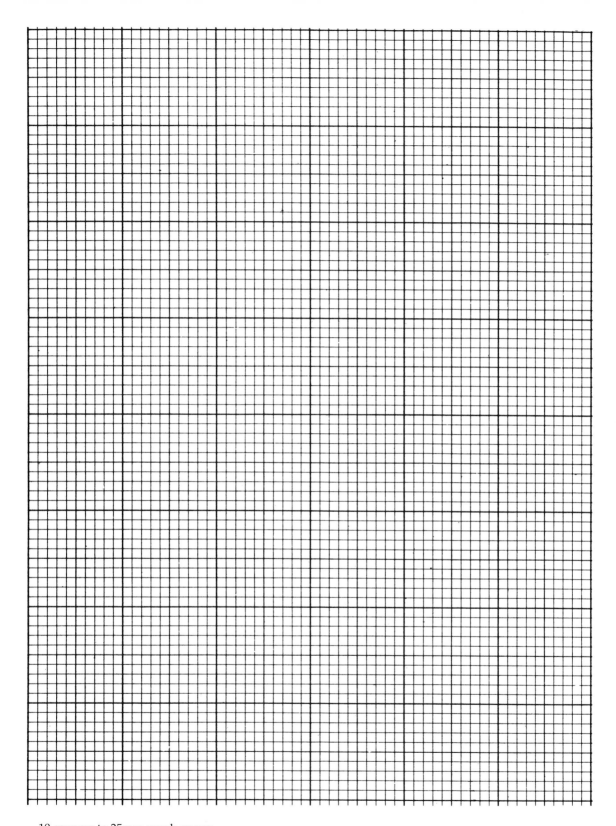

10 squares to 25mm graph paper.

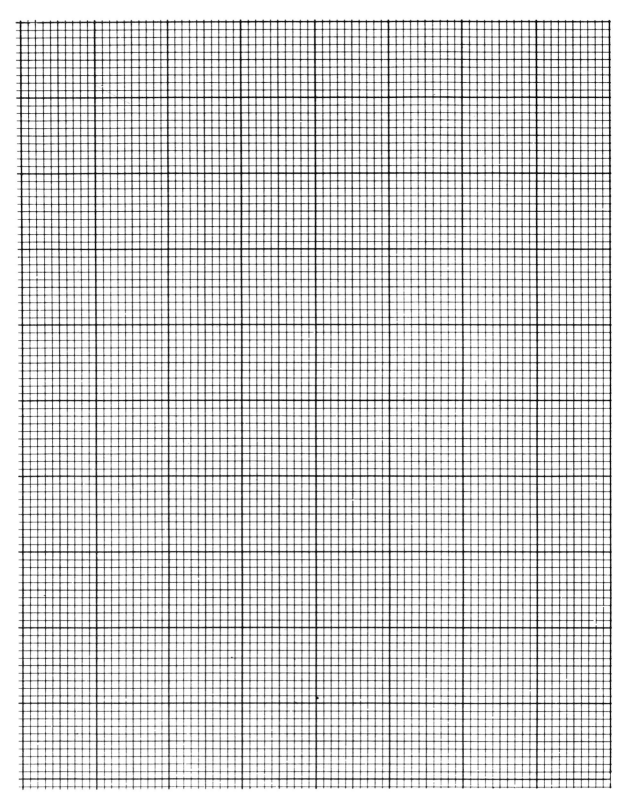

2mm graph paper.

164

Round grid with 144 dots. (Increase to the
size you want using the formula in Chapter
10.)

Glossary

There are variations in the meaning of some terms. Make sure that you understand what is meant by individual writers.

Cover the Pin After placing the pin, enclose it with another stitch using the same pairs. The second stitch is usually the same as the first. An exception is Dieppe ground.

Footside This is the straight edge of the lace which is attached to the fabric. It is worked on the right-hand side of the lace in Britain, with the exception of Downton Lace which is worked on the left in the continental manner. Directions for making a Torchon footside are in Pattern 2.

Galloon Lace with two shaped edges.

Gimp A thick thread used to outline motifs in the lace. The thread can be the same colour as the lace or a contrasting colour. Metallic threads can be used. The gimp should provide a good contrast of thickness. Coton Perle 5 and 8 are both suitable sizes.

Ground The net or mesh which surrounds the decorative parts of the lace. The lines of ground are worked at an angle of 45 degrees to the vertical.

Hanging pairs on or hanging pairs astride Hanging pairs on a pin so that the outermost left-hand and right-hand bobbin are a pair on the same thread.

Hanging pairs on in order Right to left or left to right. This also means hanging pairs on a pin so that the bobbins hanging side by side are a pair.

Hanging pairs astride.

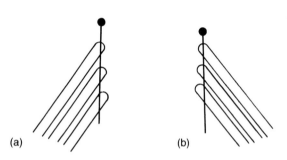

Hanging pairs in order from right to left (a) and left to right (b).

Headside The outer shaped and decorated edge.

Insertion Lace with two straight edges made to sew within the fabric.

Passives Threads which enter a motif or the headside at an angle of 45 degrees, hang vertically in the work for a time before returning to the ground at the same angle.

Setting Up Beginning a piece of lace at a suitable position on the pricking.

Support Pins Pins which hold pairs of bobbins above the setting-up line. As the pairs are taken into the lace the support

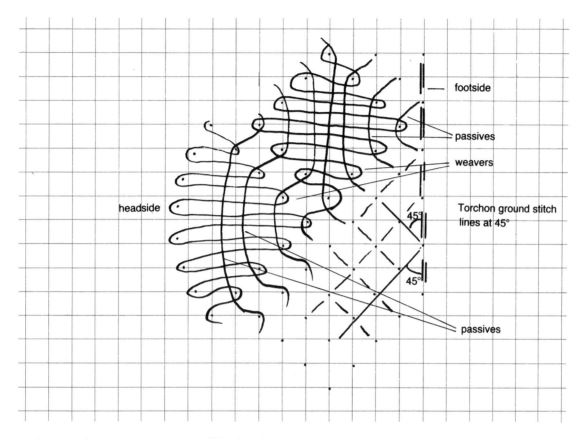

A diagram showing various parts of Torchon lace.

pins can be removed and the loops will drop down to form a neat beginning which will be the sewings line if the lace is to be joined.

Stitches The working of these stitches is explained in greater detail in the instructions for the first sample (*see* pages 43–46).

> **Whole stitch or cloth stitch** 2 over 3, 2 over 1 and 4 over 3 simultaneously, 2 over 3.
> **Half stitch or lattice stitch** 2 over 3, 2 over 1 and 4 over 3 simultaneously.
> **Twist** Pass the right-hand bobbin over the left-hand bobbin.

Cross Pass the left-hand bobbin over the right-hand bobbin.

These stitches are held in position in the pricking by pins. The stitches are worked either singly before and after a pin in the ground, or in groups in the motifs headside and footside.

Torchon motifs The decorative part within the lace.
Weavers or workers Threads which pass backwards and forwards through the passives to form the motifs.

Further Reading

BOOKS ON TORCHON LACEMAKING

Atkinson, Jane, *Pattern Design for Torchon Lace* (Batsford, 1987).
Cook, Bridget, *Torchon Lace Workbook* (Batsford, 1988).
Fisher, Jennifer, *Torchon Lace for Today* (Dryad, 1984).
Hardeman, Henk, *Torchon Lace Patterns* (Batsford, 1986).
Lewis, Robin S., *101 Torchon Patterns* (Batsford, 1988).
Nottingham, Pamela, *Techniques of Bobbin Lace* (Batsford, 1976).
Nottingham, Pamela, *Techniques of Torchon Lace* (Batsford, 1979).
Nottingham, Pamela, *Bobbin Lacemaking* (Batsford, 1983).
Stillwell, Alexandra, *Drafting Torchon Lace Patterns* (Batsford, 1986).

BOOKS ON HISTORY AND IDENTIFICATION

Bullock, Alice-Mary, *Lace and Lacemaking* (Batsford, 1981).
Earnshaw, Pat, *The Identification of Lace* (Shire, 1980).
Earnshaw, Pat, *Bobbin and Needle Laces* (Batsford, 1983).
Freeman, Charles, *Pillowlace of the East Midlands* (Luton Museum and Art Gallery, 1958).
Hopewell, Jeffery, *Pillowlace and Bobbins* (Shire, 1975).
Springett, Christine and David, *Success to the Lace Pillow* (Springett, 1981).
Springett, Christine and David, *Spangles and Superstitions* (Springett, 1987).
Reigate, Emily, *An Illustrated Guide to Lace* (Antique Collectors Club, 1986).

Useful Addresses

SUPPLIERS

In my experience, lace suppliers run a very efficient and friendly service, often sending goods by return and always willing to answer queries over the telephone. Many are lacemakers and can give advice from personal experience.

Price lists can be obtained by sending a stamped addressed envelope.

B.T. Batsford Ltd
4, Fitzhardinge Street
London
W1A 0AH
(0171 486 8484)

Publishers of a large selection of lace books. Apply to be put on their mailing list.

The Bead Society of Great Britain
c/o Carole Morris
1, Casburn Lane
Burwell
Cambridge
CB5 0ED

Doreen Campbell
Highcliff Bremilham Road
Malmesbury
Wiltshire
SN16 0DQ

A wide selection of mounts in which lace can be displayed. A selection of prickings which will fit the available frames, brooches, compacts etc.

Cobweb
c/o Mary Johnson
Tithe Farm
St Albans Road
Codicote
Hertfordshire
SG4 8UT

Antiques bobbins and lace.

Malcolm Fielding
2, Northern Terrace
Moss Lane
Silverdale
Carnforth
Lancashire
LA5 0ST

Bobbin specialist and beads.

Anita Fitzpatrick
Squirrels
16, Axeford
Chard Junction
Chard
Somerset

Block pillows in various sizes.

Framecraft Miniatures Ltd
148–150, High Street
Aston
Birmingham
B6 4US

A wide variety of frames, paperweights, jewellery, hand-mirrors etc. in which lace may be displayed.

Shirley A. Gates
Northwood
16, Harringcourt Road
Pinhoe
Exeter
Devon
EX1 8PQ

Hand-painted bobbins and other lace
supplies.

Richard Gravestock
High Wood
Crews Hill
Alfrick
Worcester
WR6 5HF

Bobbins, bobbin-winders and other
accessories made of wood.

Heffers Art and Graphics Shop
15–21, King Street
Cambridge
CB1 1LH

Blue matt transparent film.

The Honiton Lace Shop
44, High Street
Honiton
Devon
EX14 8PJ

'Rare collectors' lace from the 16th to the
20th Century'
Lacemaking equipment, threads and
books.

D.J. Hornsby
149, High Street
Burton Latimer
Kettering
Northants
NN15 5RL

A wide variety of equipment, threads,
etc. Good polystyrene mushroom
pillows.

Larkfield Crafts
Hilary Ricketts
4, Island Cottages
Mapledurwell
Basingstoke
Hampshire
RG25 2LU

A wide variety of equipment, threads and
books.

Mace and Nairn
89, Crane Street
Salisbury
Wiltshire
SP1 2PY

Threads, books and mounting fabrics.

Newnhams Lace Equipment
11, Dorchester Close
Basingstoke
Hampshire
RG23 8EX

A wide variety of lace pillows, stands, etc.
Newnhams will make pillows to personal
specifications if you have a special project
which cannot be worked on available
pillows.

Tim Parker
124, Corhampton Road
Boscombe East
Bournemouth
Dorset
BH6 5NZ

A very comprehensive range of bobbins,
threads and equipment.

J. and E. Piper
Silverlea
Flax Lane
Glemsford
Suffolk
CO10 7RS

Silk threads.

Sebalace
Waterloo Mill
Howden Road
Silsden
West Yorkshire
BD20 0HA

A wide range of equipment, threads and books.

A. Sells
Lane Cove
49, Pedley Lane
Clifton
Shefford
Bedfordshire

A wide range of equipment, threads and books.

SMP Lace
c/o Sheila Perrin
4, Garners Close
Chalfont St Peter
Buckinghamshire
SL9 0HB

A variety of pillows, pillow stands and other equipment.

Spangles
Carole Morris
1, Casburn Lane
Burwell
Cambridge
CB5 0ED

A wide variety of beads, several designs of bird cage spangles and a reproduction called 'England's Oldest Bobbin'.

C. & D. Springett
21, Hillmorton Road
Rugby
Warwickshire
CV22 5DF

Bobbin specialists. A wide variety of bits and pieces like 'angel wings' on their stalls at lace days. Several books written and published by themselves. A video on lacemaking to aid learning at home.

Ulster Crafts
115, North Main Street
Wexford
Eire

Irish linen lace threads, 'superfine' cotton lace thread.

Richard J. Viney
Unit 7
Port Royal Street
Southsea
Hampshire
PO6 4NP

Bobbins and bobbin display stands under glass domes.

AROUND THE WORLD

United States of America

Arbor House
22 Arbor Lane
Roslyn Hights
New York 11577

Beggars' Lace
P.O. Box 17263
Denver
Colorado 80217

Frivolite
15526 Densmore N
Seattle
Washington 98113

Lacis
2150 Stuart Street
Berkeley
California 9470

Van Scriver Bobbin Lace
130 Cascadilla Park
Ithaca
New York 14850

The World of Stitches
82 South Street
Milford
New Hampshire 03055

Australia

Dentelles Lace Supplies
Betty Franks
36 Lang Terrace
Northgate
Queensland 4013

Annette & John Pollard
1, Panorama Road
Penrith
New South Wales 2750

Iparra
135 Francis Street
Richmond
New South Wales 2753

West Country Lace
Shop 2
8 Dorothy Street
Leopold
Victoria 3224

The Australian Lace Guild moves to each state in turn at three-yearly intervals.

New Zealand

David Bateman Ltd
P.O. Box 100
242 North Shore Mail Centre
Auckland 10

Pauline Pease
10 Lingard Street
Christchurch

Bennett's Bookshop
38–42 P.O. Box 138
Palmerston North

The New Zealand Lace Society
10 Lingard Street
Christchurch

MUSEUMS WITH LACE COLLECTIONS

Museums in the traditional lacemaking areas in Britain probably have the best collections of lace and lacemaking equipment. Owing to lack of space much of the collection may not be displayed but can be seen if an appointment is made.

Athelstan Museum
Malmesbury
Wiltshire
(01666 822143)

Bedford Museum
Castle Lane
Bedford
MK40 3XD
(01234 353323)

Buckinghamshire Country Museum
Church Street
Aylesbury
Buckinghamshire
HP20 2QP

Castle Museum
York
YO1 1RY
(01904 653611)

Cecil Higgins Art Gallery and Museum
Castle Close
Bedford
MK40 3NY
(01234 211222)

Museum of Costume and Textiles
51, Castlegate
Nottingham
NG1 6AF
(01602 483504)

Cowper and Newton Museum
Orchard Side
Market Place
Olney
Buckinghamshire
(01234 711516)

Honiton and All Hallows Public Museum
High Street
Honiton
Devon
EX14 8PE
(01404 43851)

The Lace Centre
Severnths' Building
Castle Road
Nottingham
NG1 6AA
(01602 413539)

Luton Museum and Art Gallery
Wardown Park
Luton
Bedfordshire
LU2 7HA
(01582 746722)

Rougemont House Museum of Costume and Lace
Castle Street
Exeter
Devon
EX34 3PU
(01392 265858)

Salisbury and South Wilts Museum
The Kings House
65, The Close
Salisbury
Wiltshire
SP1 2EN
(01722 332151)

Victoria and Albert Museum
Cromwell Road
South Kensington
London
WS7 2RL
(0171 938 5000)

Many other museums probably have collections of lace. Check by writing to the curator so that you do not have a wild-goose-chase. It would also be wise to check on opening times before making a journey because many museums have limited opening hours, especially in winter.

Index

Other titles in the *Manual of Techniques* series: